PLATE I.

THE QUEEN'S PAVILION (SHALIMAR BAGH).

GARDENS OF THE GREAT MUGHALS

GARDENS OF THE GREAT MUGHALS

BY

C. M. VILLIERS STUART

GYAN

ISBN : 978-81-212-9056-2 (HB)

First Published in 1913

Indian Reprint in 2018

Published by

Gyan Publishing House
5, Ansari Road
Daryaganj, New Delhi-110002
Phone: 9811692060
E-mail: books@gyanbooks.com

Printed at: G. Print Process, Delhi.

PREFACE

THIS first sketch of the Mughal "Paradise Garden" will, I fear, make but a limited appeal to English readers, as a recollection of one of my earliest Indian experiences vividly but vainly reminds me :—On a long railway journey northward, the tedium of which had been pleasantly beguiled by a fellow-passenger's wide knowledge of the history of the country through which we were passing, the train, after thundering over a broad sandy river-bed, rushed past some buildings buried in a wood ; leaving a blurred, but entrancing vision of red enclosing walls, high tiled gateways, and slender marble minarets, rising through the densely clustering palms and forest trees of a great garden. "What is that ?" I exclaimed with delight, pressing my face to the darkened sun-proof window-pane. But here my kindly informant altogether failed me. "I really don't know," he said; " nothing much,—just one of those old Mughal baghs."

Among the many books dealing with various branches of Indian Art, it is remarkable that none have so far been devoted to the subject of Indian gardening; although, in its traditional, artistic, and symbolic aspects, the Mughal Paradise Garden supplied the leading motive in Mughal decorative art, and still underlies the whole artistic world of the Indian craftsman and builder.

This attempt to break fresh ground, this venture into the hitherto unexplored field of the Indian Garden, naturally presents great difficulties; not the least being the short time allowed me for the preparation of this volume, owing to my desire to illustrate the bearing of Indian garden-craft on the pressing problem of New Delhi, as well as on the larger subject of the Indian handicrafts. I hope, therefore, that alike my Indian and my English readers will be as lenient with me as they can.

Eastern gardens and their buildings are so closely and significantly interwoven, that the subject of architecture generally, and incidently that of New Delhi, cannot be avoided. Here in place of any words of my own, I trust I may be forgiven for repeating two well-known quotations—the first from Fergusson's Introduction to his book, *Indian Architecture*: "Architecture in India is still a living art, practised on the principles which caused its wonderful development in Europe in the twelfth and thirteenth centuries; and there, consequently, and there alone, the student of architecture has a chance of seeing the real principle of the art in action." And the shrewd Bernier's delightful dictum: "The citadel contains the Seraglio and other royal edifices; but you are not to imagine that they are such buildings as the Louvre or the Escurial. The edifices in the Fort have nothing European in their structure; nor ought they, as I have already observed, to resemble the architecture of France or Spain. It is sufficient if they have that magnificence which is suited to the climate."

Surely no "magnificence" could be more charmingly "suited to the climate" than that of an Indian garden-palace. Those who, while sympathetically inclined towards Indian art and its aims, have yet confined themselves to the beaten track in India, and would seem, therefore, to doubt the existence and genius of the Indian master-builder, will be interested in the Government Report on Modern Indian Architecture published last April. Apart from the conclusions drawn by Mr. Gordon Saunderson and Mr. J. Begg, F.R.I.B.A., Consulting Architect to the Public Works Department of the Government of India, and their recommendation of the direct employment of Indian master-builders on the score of cheapness, the photographs of the Mosque, with its purdah galleries, now under construction for Her Highness the Begam of Bhopal, and the modern merchants' houses at Bikanir and elsewhere, show that there is life and power in the native craftsmanship of India to meet and profit by any new demands we may desire to make upon it. Direct, generous, and discriminating patronage is the chief need of modern Indian art.

For the "plentiful lack" of flowers in my sketches of the old baghs, Indian garden-craft must not be held responsible. The absence of colour is mainly due to the influence of our English landscape gardeners, and their fixed belief in the universal virtue of mown grass. Happily in some Indian gardens there are still the sparkling fountains.

In the transliteration of Oriental names and words, I have, as far as possible, followed the system now in use in India. It will be familiar to English readers from Murray's Hand-book, *India, Burmah, and Ceylon.*

My grateful acknowledgments are due to Her Highness the Maji Sahiba of Bharatpur for her help in the matter of Hindu garden symbolism, and for the photographs of her Palace of Deeg; also to Her Highness Princess Bamba Duleep Singh for many details of Mughal and Sikh garden ritual and customs. I am greatly indebted to Sir George Birdwood, K.C.I.E., for his invaluable advice, and to his well-known article on *The Christmas Tree*; and to Mr. E. B. Havell for the kind loan of three articles of his on Indian gardening which appeared in *The House and Garden Magazine.*

To Mr. J. H. Marshall, C.I.E., Director-General of Archæology in India; Mr. Gordon Sanderson, Superintendent of Mohammedan and British Monuments, Northern Circle; Professor F. W. Thomas, Ph.D., Librarian of the India Office; Mr. A. G. Ellis, Assistant Librarian; and Colonel T. H. Hendley, C.I.E., I am indebted for their ready help in my search for references;

and to Dr. A. K. Coomaraswamy for his kind assistance in obtaining photographs of Mughal miniatures.

My thanks are also due to the Durbars of Kashmir and Patiala, and to Nihal Singh, Sirdar of Pinjor.

BEACHAMWELL HALL, NORFOLK,
September 1913.

CONTENTS

CHAPTER VII

CHAPTER VIII

CHAPTER IX

CHAPTER X

CHAPTER XI

CHAPTER XII

LIST OF ILLUSTRATIONS

* These Plates in colour are from water-colour drawings by the Author.

GARDEN PLANS

Printed in the Text

I saw some handfuls of the rose in bloom,
With bands of grass, suspended from a dome.
I said, " What means this worthless grass that it
Should in the rose's fairy circle sit ? "
Then wept the grass and said, " Be still ! and know
The kind their old associates ne'er forgo.
Mine is no beauty here or fragrance—true,
But in the garden of the Lord I grew."

SADI.

THE GARDENS OF THE GREAT MUGHALS

CHAPTER I

ON SOME EARLY GARDEN HISTORY

A garden enclosed—a garden of living waters,
And flowing streams from Lebanon:
Awake, O North Wind; and come thou South,
Blow upon my garden, that the spices thereof may
flow out.

Song of Songs.

A GARDEN enclosed—a garden of living waters, a garden of sweet perfumes—"that the spices thereof may flow out"—here from the *Song of Songs* are the three first motives of Indian garden-craft. First, there is the charm of contrast, that magic contrast so vivid in the East, the meeting of "the desert and the sown" at the garden's boundary walls; next, the need of running water, without which no plants or flowers could survive the fierce sunshine; and last, the motive for the moonlit garden, to

Indians the most beautiful of all, the garden of sweet perfumes and soft lights.

Indian gardening, like every other Indian art, is closely interwoven with the history of the country, and the artistic traditions and religious ideals of its designers played a far larger part in the ordering and planting of the gardens than is usual in European pleasure-grounds. Many of us have seen and admired the great terraces, canals, and tanks of the ruined Mughal gardens of Upper India and Kashmir, beautiful even in their present uncared-for state, their vast plan and solid building surviving in defiant grandeur past neglect and devastation. But few English people seem to be aware how close was the relation of these Eastern gardens, where not only the general design but each flower and tree had originally its symbolic meaning and method of arrangement, to the life and traditions of their builders.

To understand and appreciate any phase of Eastern art, its underlying symbolism must always be kept in view. The Mughals and Hindus, like other Eastern nations, were interested in art and enjoyed beauty, not for its own sake but for the religious and other traditional ideas which it represented. This essentially religious outlook is so far removed from the self-conscious art of present-day Europe, which sets so much store on the individuality of the artist, that it is not surprising to find many English people to whom Eastern insight, as expressed in Indian art, is quite unintelligible and consequently uninteresting; and this misunderstanding has been one of the chief factors in the neglect and decay of Indian national crafts. The phrase "art for art's sake" would be quite incomprehensible and meaningless to an Eastern craftsman—"art for art's sake," a catchword which curiously enough was often used, not so long ago, in connection with the then newly studied arts of China and Japan, showing how at first only the decorative value of these works appealed to Western people; the mere beauty or strangeness of the surface hiding their inner meaning, so that the motives which inspired their creation passed unnoticed.

From very early times flowers and plants have been admired and cultivated in India. There are many references to gardens in the old Buddhist literature and the Sanskrit plays. The sacred groves round the Buddhist shrines were no doubt among the earliest forms of gardening, which in later times and in moister climates developed into the well-known charming landscape styles of China and Japan.

But it was from the North, from Central Asia and Persia, that the splendid garden traditions were introduced into India, taking root there under the various Mohammedan conquerors and developing into a native style which culminated in the beautiful Kashmir Gardens built by the Mughal Emperor Jahangir and his Persian wife, the Empress Nur-Jahan.

The Afghans and Pathans showed themselves magnificent builders, as their massive forts and mosques attest. Some of the grandest and most beautiful buildings in India belong to this period, but their surrounding gardens have nearly all disappeared. Those were troublous times ; kings rose and fell with astonishing rapidity, dynasties were no sooner founded than they became extinct, and internecine wars and quarrels left little of the peace and leisure garden-craft demands. Still the comparatively long reign of Feroz Shah from 1351 to 1388 proved more peaceful than those of his predecessors, and a tradition survives of the hundred gardens that he built round Delhi—or rather round Ferozabad, as the Delhi of his day was named. Of all the hundred gardens, to-day not one is left. All their fountains, tanks, and terraces are gone, merged into the sandy plains that sweep up to the ruined walls of the city the gardens once surrounded; but throughout Northern India there remain many old canals dating from the time of Feroz Tughluk. Nearly two centuries later, in the year 1526, Mahomet Babar made his final conquest of Northern India, and fixing on Agra as his capital, commenced among other buildings the construction of the Ram Bagh on the banks of the Jumna, the earliest Mughal garden, as far as I know, still existing in India.

In Persia and Turkestan the art of building irrigated gardens was at that time very fully developed, and had behind it an ancient history and long unbroken traditions.

The writings of the early Persian poets, so full of evident delight in the flowers and gardens of their day, are well known in Europe: the Gulistans—rose gardens—of Sadi bloomed long ago—almost two hundred years before Chaucer's "sweitie roses rede" scented the summer air. "The Rose Garden" is the actual title of the poet Sadi's most famous work, and in his preface he writes :—

" Mature consideration as to the arrangements of the book made me deem it expedient that this delicate garden, and this densely wooded grove should, like Paradise, be divided into eight parts in order that it may become the less likely to fatigue."

These eight parts or terraces, being taken from the Paradise-garden of the Koran, were always the ideal for the perfect garden. " God Almighty first planted a garden," and the early followers of the Prophet, stern materialists as they were, in spite of their poets, took their ideas of Paradise very literally from the gardens around them.

Hafiz is another sweet singer through whose songs the beauteous gardens of Shiraz are well known; and that great poet of East Persia, Omar Khayyám of Korassán, is more popular now, after the lapse of nearly eight centuries, than he was in his own time and country.

One of his pupils, Khwajah Nizami of Samarcand, relates how he often used to hold conversations with his teacher in a garden ; and one day the master said to him, " My tomb shall be in a spot where the north wind may scatter the roses over it"; and adds Khwajah Nizami, "I wondered at the words he spoke, but I knew that his were no idle words. Years after, when I chanced to visit Naishapur, I went to his final resting-place, and lo! it was just outside a garden, and trees laden with fruit stretched their boughs over the garden wall, and dropped their flowers upon his tomb, so that the stone was hidden under them."

These fragrant Gardens of the Bulbul and the Rose, and all the poetic imagery they inspired, are well known to us, but the passionate national love of flowers, of which these writings were the outcome, is not so widely understood. Japan is now always thought of as the country where flowers and gardens play the largest part in the national life and art, while the parallel case of Persia is almost forgotten. This is not surprising when one reflects that in Japan garden-culture flourishes as a living art whose results are apparent to every traveller, while in Persia years of warfare and misgovernment have left the old gardens neglected and almost inaccessible.

Intense appreciation of flowers seems to have been very general all over Central Asia, and may be traced to the two great influences which underlie all national arts—climate and religion.

Nowhere in the world, perhaps, is spring more wonderful than in the high tableland of Persia and the mountainous countries lying east and west of it. Nowhere, certainly, are there such contrasts of climate: summer's heat and winter's cold alternately strip the country bare of colour, but spring pays for all: a brief spring, —only a few weeks,—into which is crowded all the flowering season of the year with a wealth of bloom hardly to be realised in more equable climates such as England and Japan, where the gardens flower on gaily for many months in succession.

In Persia as the snows melt, their whiteness is rivalled by the delicate sprays of early fruit blossoms as seen across the dark background of the cypress trees; while the pink mist of almond and apricot flowers shows in little patches of colour against the bare hillsides. Soon the ground under the trees is carpeted with bulbs, scillas, tulips, crown-imperials, narcissus, hyacinth, fritillaries, and iris. Take up a box of old Kashmiri lacquer-work and see how the flowers and colours crowd together. Lilac, jasmine, and carnations follow; then, last and best of all, come the roses, giant bushes covered with huge, pink, fragrant flowers, such masses as are seen in Europe only in the pictures of some fairy tale. White roses too, and red and yellow; but the pink roses were always the artist's favourites. For a few weeks longer the gardens and hillsides are at their brightest; then the petals fall, as summer comes and burns the land into one unending dusty monotone.

Summer flowers! There are no such things outside the carefully tended gardens.

This concentration of growth and beauty into a brief period deeply affected the imagination of the people, and all their arts reflect the national love of flowers. No wonder, then, that all the Persian poets join with old Omar in his lament, "Alas, that Spring should vanish with the rose!"

The other great influence, that of religion, is explained by the restrictions of the Koran, which forbade the delineation of human beings or animals, so that the artists of the faithful were confined to floral or geometrical designs. The Shiah sect of Aryan Persia never held very closely to this restriction, and painted men and animals freely; but flowers, fruit, and foliage remained the chief motives on the tiles and carpets for which they are so famous, lending to their work a greater beauty and interest than appears in that of their stricter Sunni brethren of Bagdad, Cairo, and Damascus, with whom geometrical designs were most in favour.

Old as these first Mohammedan gardens were, Zoroastrian skill in garden-craft takes the story back still further. To this day the gardens of the Parsees in India and the Gabres in Persia are notable for their wealth of flowers and the skill with which the plants are grown—and may we not trace in thought these gardens back through the great platforms and terraces of Persepolis, to the hanging gardens of Babylon itself? In the East ideas and forms change slowly when they change at all. This much is certain, that in all this country of Central Asia the first condition must always have been the life-giving water.

The spirit of the garden-paradises of Europe hides in the flowers, the grass, the trees, but the soul of an Eastern garden lies in none of these: it is centred in the running water which alone makes its other beauties possible. Solomon's "garden of running water" is still an actual reality. Thus the need of irrigation dictated the whole plan and arrangement of these Eastern enclosures, and herein they differ from the great Italian gardens, with which, at first sight, they seem to have so much in common. This resemblance is most striking where a hilly situation has been made use of, as in the Nishat Bagh, which rises in grand imposing terraces from the shores of the Dal Lake in Kashmir; but while in the villa gardens of Italy the beautiful fountains and waterfalls are only one of the principal adornments, in these Eastern baghs the water is the very life and soul, the *raison d'être*, of the garden itself.

A very good account of one of these Persian gardens is given in a book edited by Major P. M. Sykes, and called *The Glory of the Shia World*, in which the arrival of a Vakil-ul-Mulk and his entertainment at Mahun are thus described: "However, thanks be to Allah, the garden at Mahun was fitted to receive even such a distinguished guest as the Vakil-ul-Mulk; and, since it is one of the famous gardens of Persia, itself a land of most famous gardens, it is right that I should describe its beauties to you.

"We Persians, whenever possible, build our gardens on a gentle slope; and the garden I am describing was so constructed that two streams of crystal-like water met in the front of the building and formed an immense lake, on the surface of which numerous swans, geese, and ducks disported themselves.

"Below this lake there were seven waterfalls, just as there are seven planets; and below these again there was a second lake of smaller dimensions, and a superb gateway decorated with blue tiles.

"Perhaps the reader may think that this was all; but no, not only in the lakes, but also between the waterfalls, jets of water spouted up into the air so high that the falling spray resembled masses of diamonds. And often, when reclining in the beautiful tiled room, the plash of the jets of water and the murmur of the stream hurrying down the terraced garden between rose bushes, backed by weeping willows, planes, acacias, cypresses, and every other description of tree, have moved me strangely; and I have wept from pure joy, and then have been lulled to sleep by the overpowering sense of beauty and the murmur of the running water.

"By Allah! I think, indeed, that this garden is not surpassed in beauty by even that famous garden mentioned in the Koran:—

> 'The Garden of Iram, adorned with lofty pillars,
> The like of which hath not been created in the World.'"

Two other traits peculiar to these old Persian gardens may be remarked: the one of so constructing the canals and tanks as to keep the water brimming to the level of the paths on either hand; the other, a charming custom of paving the shallow watercourses with brilliant blue tiles, the clear rivulets running in and out between the gloom of the old cypress avenues reflecting even a deeper blue than the cloudless sky above them.

The Mughal gardens, copied from the earlier gardens of Turkestan and Persia, are invariably square or rectangular in shape, their area being divided into a series of smaller square parterres. A high wall, adorned with serrated battlements and pierced by a lofty entrance gateway, encircles the garden. These imposing entrances are a great feature of the Mughal style, and in the larger gardens there are always four main gateways, one in the centre of each wall, while the angles of the outer walls are marked by small octagonal buildings.

The water runs in a trim stone- or brick-edged canal down the whole length of the enclosure, falling from level to level in smooth cascades, or rushing in a tumult of white foam over carved water-chutes (chaddars). Below many of these waterfalls the canal flows into a larger or smaller tank, called a hauz, usually studded with numerous small fountains. The principal pavilion was often placed in the centre of the largest of these sheets of water, forming a cool, airy retreat from the rays of the midday sun, where the inmates of the garden might be lulled to sleep by the roar of the cascades, while the misty spray of the fountains, drifting in through the arches of the building, tempered the heat of a burning noontide: water pavilions, such as the exquisite black marble baradari in the harem garden of the Kashmir Shalimar, or the octagonal building which once adorned the great tank of the ruined garden at Bijbehara. In nearly all the larger gardens side-canals were added, leading out from the principal tanks and terminating in architectural features such as baradaris built into the wall, raised platforms, or gateways. From these stone-bordered canals and tanks the water required for irrigating the soil is conducted by pipes concealed beneath the ground to points where it is needed.

The trees were planted to carry out and emphasise the general lines of the garden very much as is described in the garden of Mahun, where the planes and cypress trees formed the background to the rose bushes and flowers bordering the stream. Round the outer walls also avenues of trees were planted, while the square plots intersected by the watercourses were filled with fruit trees and elaborate parterres of flowers. There were shady walks, pergolas of vines and flowers; here and there were open squares of turf shaded by large trees planted at the corners, or having one central chenar or mango tree surrounded by a raised platform of masonry or grass, which formed a free space for feasts and gatherings such as the Mughals loved. Here they could recline at ease on the soft turf, or, seated on brilliant carpets, enjoy the charm of conversation and the hookah, and indulge in musical parties, or while away the cool evenings with recitations from the favourite

Persian and Turki poets, or by chanting rhymes of their own devising, such as Babar's first ghazel (ode), which, he tells us, he composed under the chenars of the garden of Burak :—

> "I have found no faithful friend in the world but my soul,
> Except my own heart I have no trusty confidant."

The Emperor Babar laid out and improved many of the gardens round Kabul, some of which he describes at length in his Memoirs—the Bagh-i-Vafa (the Garden of Fidelity) being mentioned by him more than once. "Opposite to the fort of Adinahpur, to the south, on rising ground, I formed a char-bagh in the year 1508. It is called Bagh-i-Vafa. It overlooks the river, which flows between the fort and the palace. In the year in which I defeated Behar Khan and conquered Lahore and Dibalpur, I brought plantains and planted them here. They grew and thrived. The year before I had also planted sugar-cane in it, which throve remarkably well. I sent some of them to Badakhshan and Bokhara. It is on an elevated site, and enjoys running water, and the climate in the winter season is temperate. In the garden there is a small hillock, from which a stream of water, sufficient to drive a mill, incessantly flows into the garden below. The

PLATE II.

BAGH-I-VAFA. (THE GARDEN OF FIDELITY.)

(*By kind permission of Messrs. Luzac.*)

PLATE III.

four-fold field-plot of the garden is situated on this eminence. On the south-west part of this garden is a reservoir of water twenty feet square, which is wholly planted round with orange trees; there are likewise pomegranates. All around the piece of water the ground is quite covered with clover. This spot is the very eye of the beauty of the garden. At the time the orange becomes yellow, the prospect is delightful. Indeed the garden is charmingly laid out. To the south of this garden lies the Koh-i-Sefid (the White Mountain of Nangenhar), which separates Bangash from Nangenhar. There is no road by which one can pass it on horse-back."

These Memoirs were written by Babar in his terse native Turki; it is interesting to find his grandson, the great Akbar, requesting the scholar Mirza Abdal-Rahun to translate them into Persian while the Court was on a progress to Kashmir and Kabul, the latter country the scene of so many of the adventures and fair gardens described in the Tuzuk of Babar.

All the best caligraphists and artists, whom the catholic taste of the art-loving Akbar had drawn around him, were employed to illuminate copies of this work. The double illustration,

3

Plates II. and III., portrays two of these pages, on which the first visit of the Emperor Babar to the Bagh-i-Vafa is described. The painting is signed Bishandas, the Persian form of Vishandas, showing the artist to have been Hindu. In this miniature Babar is seen to be personally directing the laying-out of "the four-fold field-plot." Two gardeners hold the measuring line, the architect with his plan stands in attendance, while the tank, somewhat reduced in size, is fitted into the bottom corner of the picture. Pomegranates and orange trees border the square plot, and above the walls tower the snowy heights of the White Mountain, on which, to show its altitude, the artist introduces an ibex, with chikor (mountain partridge) on the lower slopes. An embassy of the Begs knocks at the garden gate, hastening, no doubt, with news of some fresh revolt or trouble in the camp: but the Emperor, completely absorbed in his favourite pastime, is not to be diverted from his new garden schemes.

Fifteen years afterwards Babar mentions another visit to this favourite spot: three days' rest snatched from the midst of his endless campaigns against the turbulent Afghans. The garden had matured, and his naïve delight in the beauty and success of his schemes and plantations is very charming. "Next morning I reached the Bagh-i-Vafa; it was the season when the garden was in all its glory. Its grass-plots were all covered with clover; its pomegranate trees were entirely of a beautiful yellow colour. It was then the pomegranate season and the pomegranates were hanging red on the trees. The orange trees were green and cheerful, loaded with innumerable oranges; but the best oranges were not yet ripe. Its pomegranates were excellent, though not equal to the fine ones of our country. I was never so much pleased with the Garden of Fidelity as on this occasion." A little further on the Emperor adds: "As I had an intention of travelling through the Lemghan in the winter, I desired them to save about twenty orange trees around the piece of water for my use."

The second illustration given of this garden is taken from another copy of the Memoirs, now in the British Museum, and shows the sugar-cane and plantains which had been brought from Lahore with such care; gardeners busily digging and sowing seeds in the little plots of ground between the water channels, and a small copper fountain of a primitive type is playing in the centre of the tank.

Apart from the main system of irrigation, it is curious to notice from these old accounts and miniatures how in many ways the Mughal gardens of the sixteenth century resembled those of Tudor England. These English gardens, alas! have nearly all vanished, their last vestiges swept away by the sham romanticism of the eighteenth century and the zeal of those who followed the traditions of the once-lauded landscape gardener, "Capability" Brown. One by one the magnificent old gardens of the great houses were destroyed, but a glance at nearly any of the plans shown in Kip's drawings of famous English halls and castles, published in 1707, will prove how much the old English and Indian gardens had in common. Two centuries earlier a still closer affinity can be seen in the garden backgrounds of the illuminations in a Flemish manuscript of the Roman de la Rose. In both styles the garden was confined by high boundary walls, and in both the whole scheme of house and garden, buildings and planting, were treated throughout in definite relation to each other. Towers in the east, and garden houses in the west were an invariable feature marking the corners of the walls. The cistern fountains in the European illuminations might have played in the Garden of Fidelity; the "pleached allies" and "proper knots" of English gardens were the vine pergolas and geometrical parterres of the Mughals; while their central baradaris or raised chabutras (platforms) answered the same purpose as the banqueting hall on the "mound," without which at one time no English noble's garden was complete.

The question of the park was different. The old English engravings usually depict walled gardens surrounded by a large, and more or less wild, deer-park, through which ran avenues extending the main lines of the garden. The Mughals, on the other hand, had no need of outer enclosures for preserving game while the primeval forests and jungles still clothed the hillsides, so that their great chenar and mango avenues were generally placed within the garden walls. The space which these walls enclosed was a large one, 600 yards by 400 yards being a very usual size, while many of the Mughal baghs were on a much bigger scale than this. In these large baghs the actual flower garden may be said to be confined to the lines of the principal canals and the squares which bordered on them, the sides of the garden being treated more like a park and planted with large avenues of trees under which tents could be pitched.

Many of the royal gardens owed their origin to the fact that they were specially designed to accommodate the Court on the constant royal progresses entailed by the vast size of the Empire. Where there was no garden kept in readiness against the coming of the Emperor even the temporary camp was carefully pitched with that regard for form, combined with a beautiful site, of which the Mughals were so mindful. Bernier, the French physician, travelling in the train of the Emperor Aurungzeb to Kashmir, mentions how "one of the Peeche-Kanes has no sooner reached the place intended for the new encampment than the grand Quartermaster selects some fine situation for the King's tents, paying, however, as much attention as possible to the exact symmetry of the whole camp. He then marks out a square, each side of which measures more than three hundred ordinary paces. A hundred pioneers presently clear and level this space, raising square platforms of earth on which they pitch the tents. The whole of this extensive square is then encompassed with kanates or screens. The kanates are made of strong cloth lined with printed Indian calico, representing large vases of flowers."

There are many who seem to think that this love of form and beauty, so ingrained in the Mughal character, found its only outlet and was alone displayed in the royal gardens, forts, and palaces. This was hardly the case in India any more than it has been in Europe, though in every clime art flourishes most vigorously when to the inspirations of race and religion a personal stimulus is added. In Mughal times it was a pious act to plant avenues of trees to shade the wayfarers on the great high-roads. Gardens, and orchards too, were founded by private persons for the public benefit, very much after the manner of our old English foundations and almshouses. Town planning, about which there has been so much talk in England of recent years, was an art carried out on a grand scale by the great Emperors of India and Persia; and I doubt if New Delhi, even when finished, will contain anything so fine as the Chenar Bagh,

1350 yards long, "down the centre of which ran a channel of water falling in terraces and collecting here and there in large shallow basins wherein fountains played; where on either side the channel was an avenue of trees and a paved footway for pedestrians, and beyond this again ran another avenue and a raised causeway, for horses and vehicles, against the flanking walls." Such was the approach which Shah Abbas, the equally magnificent and art-loving contemporary of Shah Jahan, created for his beloved Persian capital, Ispahan.

The grand old terrace gardens of India and Kashmir lie for the most part forlorn and neglected, or so changed that nearly all their charm and character are lost. This is strange when these large water-gardens have so much in common with their European contemporaries, the Italian gardens of the sixteenth and seventeenth centuries—the vast pleasure-grounds in the building of which the Cardinals and Princes of the Renaissance vied with each other, piling up those wondrous terraces overlooking the blue rolling waves of the Roman Campagna, or crowning the heights of Fiesole above the quiet beauty of the Arno valley, where the brown towers and dark cypress spires rise through the silver mist of olive trees. When these Italian gardens are so much admired, photographed, and visited, why are the Mughal baghs of the Indian foot-hills and the great gardens of the Dal Lake forgotten, and Indian garden-craft as a whole ignored?

I am speaking now of garden-design, gardening in its artistic sense, for gardening in a horticultural sense still flourishes in India. It is best to be quite clear about these two aspects of garden-craft. One may be regarded as the building of the house, the other as the furnishing. One is the art of building and planning for all time and for all generations; the other the art wherewith each generation in its turn replants according to its pleasure. Speaking strictly, horticulture is not an art at all, but only the science of improving form and flavour, scent and colour, and is quite apart from the garden-craft which afterwards can in combination and arrangement make use of such knowledge with artistic skill.

Naturally in a scientific age, the scientific side of gardening makes the first appeal; but both aspects are equally important, and it is the common confusion of these two quite separate ideas which has gone far to destroy European garden-design.

An old Indian garden-palace built for the hot weather offers a perfect illustration of harmony of house and garden. For a time I stayed in just such a place, situated far away in the country of the Himalayan foot-hills; a huge walled enclosure, partly fortified. First came the great high gateway which formed the double purpose of entrance hall and quarters for the guard; beyond extended a large flower garden laid out in parterres beside the stream, at the end of which was the men's dining-room. On its other side this building opened on to the rose garden, on the far side of which towered the high palace of the women's quarters, with its delightful roof bedrooms. Here, built into the side walls, a kitchen pavilion on the one hand balanced rooms for guests on the other; while forty feet below lay the large fruit garden, the "bostand," with the summer drawing-room delightfully placed in the centre of the largest fountain tank.

Though the beauty of design and the charm of garden symbolism have been lost sight of in India, botanical gardens and horticultural colleges are always improving well-known shrubs and flowers and acclimatizing new ones, and their actual cultivation appeals keenly to nearly every one, and especially to Anglo-Indians. Indeed, I should say that the average Englishman in India takes a far more practical interest in his garden there than he would do at home in England. The rapid growth and beauty of the strange new flowers and trees attract him; while life is spent so much out of doors, that the garden plays a larger part and the house a much smaller one than they do with us in colder countries.

What cause, then, in latter-day India has led to this divorce of horticulture and design? Why is "the art, so well understood by the Mughals, of planning and planting gardens in direct harmonious relation to the house, palace, or mausoleum to which they belong, now rarely if ever practised?"

There are two main causes which have contributed to the neglect of Indian garden-craft. The first is the obvious change of habits and manners. The railway train brings the cool hill station within comparatively easy reach. There is no need now for the long journeys of the Court to Kashmir,—such journeys as the Emperor Jahangir and his consort, the famous

Nur-Jahan Begam (better known as Nur-Mahal), undertook no less than thirteen times, crossing the snowy passes of the Pir Panjal on elephants —a strange and dangerous undertaking. These adventures, however, were for the Court alone; for most people a garden close to the city walls took the place of hill stations and summer resorts. Every omrah (noble) and rich man made one or more of these gardens, with running water, fountains, and cool, airy pavilions in which to take refuge from the stifling summer heat of the great white city palaces. Running water was the essential feature of these gardens. Even the city palace had its fountain and inner court planted with shrubs and flowers for the special use of the ladies of the zenana. Bernier, writing from the Court of Aurungzeb at Delhi, mentions that the garden-houses of the omrahs, "though mostly situated on the banks of the river and in the suburbs, are yet scattered in every direction. In these hot countries a house is considered beautiful if it be capacious, and if the situation be airy and exposed on all sides to the wind, especially the northern breezes. A good house has its courtyards, gardens, trees, basins of water, small *jets d'eau* in the hall or at the entrance, and handsome subterraneous apartments which are furnished with large fans, and on account of their coolness are fit places for repose from noon until four or five o'clock, when the air becomes suffocatingly warm. Instead of these cellars many persons prefer kas-kanays, that is, small and neat houses made of straw or odoriferous roots, placed commonly in the middle of a parterre so near to a reservoir of water that the servants may easily moisten the outside by means of water brought in skins. They consider that a house to be greatly admired ought to be situated in the middle of a large flower garden, and should have four divan-apartments raised the height of a man from the ground, and exposed to the four winds, so that the coolness may be felt from any quarter. Indeed, no handsome dwelling is ever seen without terraces on which the family may sleep during the night. They always open into a large chamber into which the bedstead is easily moved in case of rain, when thick clouds of dust arise, when the cold air is felt at break of day, or when it is found necessary to guard against those light but penetrating dews which frequently cause a numbness in the limbs and induce a species of paralysis."

Nothing could be more charming or more suited to the climate than these country houses round Delhi as seen by Bernier in 1660, and the ill-adapted, modern Anglo-Indian bungalows, with their sloping roofs, haphazard-shaped compounds, and dusty gardens open to the public gaze, cannot be said to be a great advance in appropriateness or taste.

The second cause which led to the decline of Indian gardening was less obvious but more destructive. It was the introduction of the English landscape garden, *le Jardin Anglais*, of the eighteenth century, "the mock wild garden" which surrounded the English classic houses of that period. This change was a revolt of the garden alone against some of the final absurdities of the Dutch designs and a lifeless formalism which had become dreary, a change which may be partly traced to the East, for it was to some extent inspired by travellers' tales of the landscape gardens of China and Japan.

All styles have their weak points, which in the end bring about their decadence and make for change. In Europe, Gothic architecture, degenerating in France to a riot of flamboyant curves, made the renaissance of the severer classical lines a welcome relief. The classical formality, at first so charming in its restrained yet decorative outlines of house and garden, in its turn sank to decadence after the period of Versailles, where, to quote from Sir George Sitwell's most valuable book, *On the Making of Gardens,*—a book with no direct reference to the East, yet so full of suggestion and imaginative sympathy with beauty in every form that one wishes it might be the text-book of every garden-maker, whether in England or in India—" The long drawn-out monotony of the new style, which took no account of the genius of the place, but sought everywhere to overwhelm nature, was bound to provoke a reaction. As under Louis XIV. the garden had encroached upon the park so now the park swept back over the garden, bringing the one unending sweep of the bare English lawn up to the very windows of the house. . . . The garden was deprived first of its boundaries and then of its flowers, sham rivers, dead trees, and broken bridges were planted in appropriate positions, while over the country-side in the neighbourhood of the great houses there broke out a dreadful eruption of Gothic temples and Anglo-Saxon keeps, Corinthian arches and Druid amphitheatres, of classic urns, Chinese pagodas and Egyptian pyramids, all with inscriptions in Greek or black-letter appealing to the eye of taste and the tear of sensibility."

We may, however, place to the credit of the English landscape style the broad treatment of parks, the skilful management of large sheets of water, and the effective grouping of trees; but these were more than counterbalanced by the destruction of the garden near the house, till all that was ultimately left of the once charming walled pleasance had shrunk into an ugly kitchen garden, unconnected with the house, hiding its necessarily "formal" walls in a neighbouring wood, where hideous greenhouses and untidy, odd potting sheds replaced the stately orangery and the corner garden towers of former days. Such was the garden-craft we brought to India when the fine old Anglo-Indian houses of Madras and Calcutta were in process of building!

For whatever we may think of their gardens, the eighteenth-century classical buildings in India were good of their kind and adapted to the climate. But as the English houses grew more formal and severely classical, the gardens, as if

PLATE IV.

British Museum.

"THE GARDEN WAS IN ALL ITS GLORY." (BABAR.)

in protest, lost all form, and the fundamental principle of the relation between house and garden was completely lost sight of—the principle till then so strictly adhered to throughout all the periods of English art. Such was the havoc which this fashion wrought that even to-day in England we have not altogether recovered in our gardens this lost sense of harmony.

CHAPTER II

GARDENS OF THE PLAINS—AGRA

Each Morn a thousand Roses brings, you say;
Yes, but where leaves the Rose of Yesterday?
And this first Summer month that brings the Rose
Shall take Yamshýd and Kaikobad away.

OMAR KHAYYÁM.

FAR away to the northward of the sunbaked plains of Agra, beyond the great snow barrier of the Himalayas, lies the small kingdom of Ferghana—"on the borders of the habitable world," as Babar, Prince of Gardeners, shortly describes his native valleys on the opening page of his inimitable Memoirs.

With the advent of the Emperor Zehireddin Mohammed, called Babar (the Tiger), the history of garden-design in India may be said to begin; and throughout his Memoirs, the record of thirty-five years spent in almost incessant warfare, there are repeated references to flowers and gardens.

In the midst of long accounts of wars and skirmishes we find the Emperor hurrying back to Kàbul to see how his Garden of Felicity had prospered. Wherever he went, he paused to note the flowers, birds, and animals that were new to him. Marching through the mountains of Ghurbend in Afghanistan Babar observes that: "The ground is richly diversified by various kinds of tulips. I once directed them to be counted, and they brought in thirty-two or thirty-three different sorts of tulips. There is one species which has a scent in some degree like a rose, and which I termed *laleh-gul-bui*, (the rose-scented tulip). This species is found only in the Sheikh's Plain, in a small spot of ground, and nowhere else. In the skirts of the same hills, below Perwan, is produced the Hundred-leaved tulip, which is likewise found only in one narrow spot of ground, as we emerge from the straits of Ghurbend." This last flower, which Babar mistook for a tulip, is really the double red poppy.

The Emperor gives a long list of many beautiful gardens surrounding Samarkand at the time of his first visit to that city. The Perfect Garden, the Heart-delighting, and the Garden of the Plain are among those he mentions as adorned

PLATE V.

EVENING IN THE GARDENS OF THE TAJ.

with elaborate garden-houses and pillared halls. These were royal gardens, but "in the time of Sultan Ahmed Mirza," Babar's uncle, "many of the greater and lesser Begs formed gardens, some large, others small. Among these, the Chehar Bagh of Dervish Muhamed Terkhan, in respect of climate, situation, and beauty, is equalled by few. It is situated lower down than the Garden of the Plain, on a small eminence that rises above the valley of Kulbeh, and commands a view of the whole vale, which stretches out below. In this Chehar Bagh there is a variety of different plots laid out one above another, all on a regular plan, and elms, cypresses, and white poplars planted in the different compartments. It is a very perfect place. Its chief defect is that it has no great stream of running water."

Babar's love of flowers and gardens would seem to have been as much a national as a personal characteristic. To this day the far-off towns of Eastern Turkestan are celebrated for their orchards. Sir Aurel Stein, in his account of his adventurous journey to the sand-buried cities of Khotan, constantly mentions the gardens which formed such pleasant camping-grounds all along his route from Kashmir to his headquarters at Khotan. At Yarkand, the garden reserved for him, the Chini Bagh, "proved quite a summer palace within a large walled-in garden." And again, "When alone in my temporary mansion, I felt the reality of the charms which such an abode offers even more than I had in the old Mughal and Sikh garden-residences, once my favourite haunts in the campagna of Lahore."

Tanks filled with the sacred lotus flowers figured largely in many of the fresco paintings uncovered among the ruined cities north of Khotan, and adjoining one of the buried houses the outlines of an ancient garden were distinctly traceable. House and garden had lain buried under the drifting sand for nearly 1600 years when Sir Aurel Stein first discovered them. "The trunks of the poplars, which still rise eight to ten feet from the original surface, and are thus clearly visible above the sand-drift, are grouped in the same little squares, and enclosing rectangular avenues which can be seen in every well-kept Bostan (orchard) from Kashgar to Keriya."

Babar, after his final conquest of Northern India in the year 1526, fixed on his new capital at Agra, where one of his first concerns was the carrying out of the old Turki traditions in the building of an Imperial char-bagh (garden-palace, literally " four gardens "). At Agra, however, the flat character of the country afforded little scope for planning a fine garden, such as the great terraced enclosures of Samarkand or the Kabul Hills.

The Hindus themselves, at that time, appear to have lost much of their earlier taste for gardening and the skill which characterised the Indian Buddhist monks, and to have done little more than plant groves of trees round the tanks constructed to catch the summer rains, making no effort to irrigate such gardens as existed. This lack of irrigation struck the new Emperor of India very forcibly, accustomed as he was to the elaborate care and skill with which the fields and gardens were watered in Persia and his own country of Ferghana. " It always appears to me," he writes, " that one of the chief defects of Hindustan is the want of artificial water-courses. I had intended, wherever I might fix my residence, to construct water-wheels, to produce an artificial stream, and to lay out an elegant and regularly planned pleasure-ground.

"Shortly after coming to Agra, I passed the Jumna with this object in view, and examined the country, to pitch upon a fit spot for a garden. The whole was so ugly and detestable, that I repassed the river quite repulsed and disgusted. In consequence of the want of beauty and the disagreeable aspect of the country, I gave up my intention of making a char-bagh; but as no better situation presented itself near Agra, I was finally compelled to make the best of this same spot. First of all I began to sink the large well which supplies the baths with water; I next fell to work on the piece of ground on which are the ambli (Indian tamarind trees), and the octagonal tank; I then proceeded to form the large tank and its enclosure; and afterwards the tank and talar, or grand hall of audience, that are in front of the stone palace. I next finished the garden of the private apartments, and the apartments themselves, after which I completed the baths. In this way, going on, without neatness and without order, in the Hindu fashion, I, however, produced edifices and gardens which possessed considerable regularity. In every corner I planted suitable gardens; in every garden I sowed roses and

PLATE VI.

British Museum.

"ONE OF THE CHIEF DEFECTS OF HINDUSTAN IS THE WANT OF ARTIFICIAL WATER-COURSES." (BABAR.)

narcissus regularly, and in beds corresponding to each other. We were annoyed with three things in Hindustan: one was its heat, another its strong winds, the third its dust. Baths were the means of removing all three inconveniences. In the bath we could not be affected by the winds. During the hot winds, the cold can there be rendered so intense, that a person often feels as if quite powerless from it. The room of the bath, in which is the tub or cistern, is finished wholly of stone. The water-run is of white stone: all the rest of it, its floor and roof, is of a red stone, which is the stone of Biana. Khalifeh, Sheikh Zin, Yunis Ali, and several others, who procured situations on the banks of the river, made regular and elegant gardens and tanks, and constructed wheels after the fashion of Lahore and Debalpur, by means of which they procured a supply of water. The men of Hind, who had never before seen places formed on such a plan, or laid out with so much elegance, gave the name of Kabul to the side of the Jumna on which these palaces were built."

This long account of the building of the garden-palace at Agra gives a good illustration of the style of garden-design which the Emperor

Babar introduced into India. The Mughals, with their fine traditions, laid most stress on the choice of site. Babar was evidently too wise to suppose, as many modern garden planners suppose, that he could build a great garden without a great idea or a great opportunity; and to his disgust, the dull monotony of the plains of Agra offered neither. Water, too, was a vital necessity to cool the dwelling rooms, supply the baths, and irrigate these immense terraced enclosures. All the finest Mughal gardens or their ruins are found in beautiful situations, centring round a hillside spring, like the gardens of Achibal, Verinag, Wáh, and Pinjor; or else built across a narrow ravine or valley through which a constant stream of water flows, such as the Kashmir Shalimar Bagh, the Gardens of the Ghat near Jeypore, and older still, the ill-famed Persian gardens of the Castle of Alamut,—the Paradise of the Assassins, of which Ser Marco Polo left such a quaint description, and the crusaders brought home strange tales.

No spring or rivulet being available in the vicinity of Agra, Babar perforce had to start the work by digging wells; next, he proceeded with the tamarind tree enclosure and its octagonal tank, and then the great hall of audience. In Persia and India a house or palace is always understood to be included under the name of garden, and the whole composition was closely and beautifully interwoven. How much the finest Mughal buildings lose by the destruction or alteration of their gardens can be easily seen in the great palace-forts at Agra, Delhi, and Lahore, and the many desolate enclosures, all that are now left of the once "Paradise-like orchards" of the Moslem garden-tombs.

The Ram Bagh, on the left bank of the Jumna, may possibly be the garden-palace of Babar's description. It was a royal garden in the time of his great-grandson Jahangir; one of the numerous palaces of the Empress Nur-Jahan. It is astonishing to find how many of the famous Mughal gardens throughout Northern India and Kashmir owe their inception to, or were directly inspired by, the taste and the love of natural scenery and flowers of this royal lady, who shared with Babar the joyous art-loving traditions inherited from Turki and Persian ancestors. In the Ram Bagh the great Emperor was laid in his last sleep, before his remains were removed to their final resting-place, his favourite Garden of the New Year, near Kabul. All succeeding rulers have kept up this garden of his at Agra, and it is said to have obtained its name of Ram Bagh from the Mahrattas in the eighteenth century.

Unfortunately, the original character of these gardens is almost lost; the raids and wars of old times, and the mistaken zeal for English landscape-gardening have swept away the avenues of alternating cypress trees and fruit trees. Gone are the glowing parterres, carpets of colour —"the roses and narcissus planted regularly in beds corresponding to one another"—such as were spread to delight the eyes of Babar or Nur-Mahal. Winding drives and meaningless paths now replace the charming old formality, while the baradaris on the riverside terrace are disfigured and modernised. There remain only the terraces, fountains, and narrow watercourses, with their tiny, carved water-chutes, and the old well from which the garden was supplied with water from the Jumna.

Between the Ram Bagh and the Chini-ka-Rauza, the latter a ruined tomb, once entirely covered with an exquisite mosaic of tile work, lies the Zuhara Bagh, another large walled enclosure. This formerly contained the largest garden-palace at Agra, and belonged to Zuhara, one of Babar's daughters. A great well outside the enclosure, some 220 feet in circumference, has recently been filled up; and altogether the garden is said to have possessed no less than sixty wells.

Five and a half miles from Agra, down the great north road of Babar's planning, lies Sikandrah, the tomb of his grandson Akbar. The building stands in the midst of a vast level garden, a char-bagh of the plains. The gardens mentioned so far, those of Babar's descriptions and the garden of Mahun, were all constructed in a series of terraces on sloping ground on the usual Turki and Persian plan. The ideal pleasance, according to those traditions, was itself a symbol of life, death, and eternity, and should be divided into eight terraces, following the eight divisions of the Paradise of the Koran mentioned in the previous chapter. In other cases seven was the number chosen, to symbolise the seven planets, and the ground plan of every garden was designed in accordance with some symbolic or mystic idea. No wonder, then, that Babar was disgusted by the surroundings of his new Indian capital—the far-reaching plains and the lack of natural beauty which prevented the realisation of the great char-bagh of his dreams, the Imperial garden-palace, which, with its terraces and fountains, should rival and outshine all those on the hillsides of Kabul and Samarkand.

In these terrace pleasure-grounds the main pavilion, the climax of the garden, is in nearly every case placed either on the topmost terrace, from which wide views were visible, or else on the lowest embankment to enjoy the long vista up the line of dancing, sparkling waterfalls and fountains.

At Sikandrah a different scheme is followed, which may be taken as a type of the Mughal gardens of the plains. The plan is of extreme simplicity—the fourfold field-plot of Babar, and also the Hindu mythologised geography of the world. This was a Holy Land, with Mount Meru in its midst, from which the waters of a secret spring flow north, south, east, and west in four great fertilising streams. On the central mount grows the sacred tree, the Tree of Knowledge of Good and Evil, with Naga, the holy water-snake, the embodiment of the spring, coiled about its roots. These same ideas of the sacred mountain and the holy tree with its secret spring and guardian snake are connected with all early conceptions of a Paradise, and in every language the very word Paradise, or garden, means "enclosed." Such was the Eridu of the Assyrians; the Eden of the Jews; Mount Olympus, the Greek Garden of the Gods; the Vara or Pairidaesa of Ancient Persia, where "on the white Homa tree sits the Saena bird and shakes down from it the seeds of life, which, as they fall, are at once seen by the bird Kamros as it watches for them from the top of the heavenly mountain Hara-Berezaiti, and are carried by it, and scattered far and wide over the world." The Paradise of the Hindus was Ida-varsha, the garden of Ida, mother of mankind; there on the sacred slopes of Mount Meru grew the "Tree of Ages" and the fragrant "Tree of Every Perfect Gift." Back and ever backward through the ages this Paradise idea extends until it is lost in the beginning of all human things, the worship of the first wonders and necessities of life, the sky and the mountains, the water and the fruit-bearing trees. And still a flicker from the old tradition lingers on and lights our children's Holy Tree at Christmastide.

In early ages the tree on the mount was replaced by a temple; in Buddhist times the stone chhattravali or umbrellas, the symbols of the sacred tree and its branches, crowned the building; the idea was carried on by the Hindu temples, and with the coming of the Mohammedans the temple on the mount is replaced by the tomb or baradari on a central platform from which the four waterways still flow.

Back to such simple pieties we are led by the Hindu custom prescribing the laying out of a garden, "the purest of human pleasures," as a religious function, of which the distinctive rite is the formal marriage of the fruit trees with the garden well, two of the finest young trees being planted beside the conduit head. After which the dakshina (right-hand-going) is performed, the garden being perambulated by its planters. This marriage of the fruit trees is a favourite motive with Hindu craftsmen, and the well-known perforated stone windows in the mosque of Sidi Sayyid at Ahmedabad are among the most exquisite examples of its use.

Sikandrah is laid out on this plan of the cosmic cross, in a huge square enclosure with high battlemented walls. In the midst, raised on a wide platform, stands the mausoleum, on each side of which are tanks with central fountains supplying the water for the narrow canals which once ran down the centre of the raised stone pathways. The mausoleum was commenced by Akbar himself. Mr. Havell, in his book on Agra, draws attention to the fact that—"It is different in plan from any other Mughal monument, and, contrary to the usual Mohammedans' custom, the head of the tomb of Akbar is turned towards the rising sun, and not towards Mecca. The whole structure gives the impression of a noble but incompleted idea; both in its greatness and in its incompleteness, it is typical of Akbar and his work." The tomb of India's greatest Emperor fitly combines both Hindu and Moslem traditions. Even the present park of grass and scattered trees, crossed by the raised stone walks, preserves in bare outline something of the garden's ancient symbolism.

Numerous fine mausoleums, or their ruins, lie scattered round the three great Mughal capitals, Agra, Delhi, and Lahore, some of which still retain their enclosing garden walls. These garden-tombs were a great feature of Moslem art. It was customary for the Mughal princes

PLATE VII.

SIKANDRAH.

and omrahs to keep up various pleasure-grounds outside the cities, one of which was always chosen as the owner's last resting-place. The central baradari which had been used as the summer palace during the owner's lifetime formed the mausoleum at his death, when the garden was made over to religious purposes and its fruit usually distributed among the fakirs who tended the tomb and the many beggars and wayfarers who passed by its gates. A garden of this description must have been acquired by purchase or fair means, else its possession would entail misfortune—Babar alludes to this idea when he mentions that he paid the full price of the Bagh-i-Kilan and received a grant of it from its proprietor. This was the beautiful garden in the district of Istalif, in which he was finally buried. "Istalif," he says, "is a district full of gardens, green, gay, and beautiful," in which was a garden "called Bagh-i-Kilan, or the Great Garden, which Mugh Beg Mirza seized upon. I paid the price of the garden to the proprietors, and received from them a grant of it. A perennial stream, large enough to turn a mill, runs through the garden; and on its banks are planted planes and other trees. Formerly this stream flowed in a winding and crooked course, but I ordered its course to be altered according to a regular plan, which added greatly to the beauty of the place. Lower down than these villages, and about a kos or a kos and a half above the level plain, on the lower skirts of the hills, is a fountain, named Khwajeh-seh-yaran (Khwajeh-three-friends), around which there are three species of trees; above the fountain are many beautiful plane trees, which yield a pleasant shade. On the two sides of the fountain, on small eminences at the bottom of the hills, there are a number of oak trees; except on these two spots, where there are groves of oak, there is not an oak to be met with on the hills west of Kabul. In front of this fountain, towards the plain, there are many spots covered with the flowery arghwan tree, and besides these arghwan plots there are none else in the whole country. It is said that these three kinds of trees were bestowed on it by the power of three holy men, beloved of God; and that this is the origin of the name Seyaran. I directed this fountain" (*i.e.* spring) "to be built round with stone, and formed a cistern of lime and mortar twenty feet square. On the four sides of this fountain, a fine level platform for resting was constructed on a very neat plan. At the time when the arghwan flowers begin to blow, I do not know that any place in the world is to be compared to it. The yellow arghwan is here very abundant, and the yellow arghwan's blossom mingles with the red."

The blossoming arghwan trees (*Bauhinia variegata*) whose mingled reds and yellows so delighted Babar, were flowering shrubs; and must not be confused with the arghwan (anemone) parterres with which he was so struck in the beautiful gardens he visited on his march past Attock:—"In different beds, the ground was covered with purple and yellow arghwan flowers. On the one hand were beds of yellow flowers, in bloom; on the other hand, red flowers were in blossom. In many places they sprang up in the same bed, mingled together as if they had been flung and scattered abroad. I took my seat on a rising ground near the camp, to enjoy the view of all the flower-plots. On the six sides of this eminence they were formed as into regular beds. On one side were yellow flowers; on the other purple, laid out in triangular beds. On two other sides there were fewer flowers; but, as far as the eye

AN OFFERING TO NAGA.

could reach, there were flower gardens of a similar kind. In the neighbourhood of Peshawar, during the spring, the flower-plots are exquisitely beautiful." A judgment which still holds good, as those must agree, who, like Babar, have passed through Northern India in spring-time : the brief northern spring, when even the exposed, dusty bungalow-gardens are lit up by the wonder of the rose bushes, ending as the first blast of the burning summer winds blows out the roses' fairy lamps of red, pink, white, and yellow.

Across the river Jumna, and on the same side as the Ram Bagh, is the tomb of I'timad-ud-Daulah (the Lord High Treasurer), one of the most beautiful of all the Mughal garden-tombs. This exquisite mausoleum, the first example of inlaid marble work in a style directly evolved from the Persian tile-mosaics, was raised by the Empress Nur-Jahan to the memory of her father, Mirza Ghiyas Beg. Her remarkable Persian—or, according to another account, Turki—family, had such an influence on Mughal art during its most brilliant period that their relationships are worth remembering. Ghiyas Beg, who became the Lord High Treasurer of Jahangir and afterwards Wazir or Prime Minister, had left his home to seek his fortune at the Court of Akbar, where there were already relatives of his ; and with him came his wife, his son, and an infant daughter born on the journey to Lahore. A clever man and genial scholar, he quickly rose to power, and his little daughter, who seems to have inherited much of his ability, as well as his love for art, became in after years the famous Empress Nur-Jahan. She and her brother Asaf Khan, who, in his turn, became Wazir, completely ruled the empire in the closing days of Jahangir ; while Asaf Khan's daughter (Nur-Jahan's niece and daughter-in-law) was the Mumtaz Mahal, the Crown of the Palace, whose death inspired the building of the Taj. This tomb of the founder of the family shows plainly their influence on the art of their day, the inlaid work with its designs of vases, fruits, drinking-cups, and cypress trees repeating in marble all the familiar motives of Persian tile-mosaic.

The whole enclosure and the mausoleum seem small after the huge pile set in the vast ruined garden at Sikandrah. But though this old pleasure-ground by the riverside is carefully maintained, its empty water channels, bare mown grass-plots, and scattered trees show that the garden has quite lost its original character. The four great tanks on the central platform are dry and empty, no glittering fountain spray breaks the darkness of the doorways, nor overflows in ripples down the tiny carved water-chutes; and the empty, narrow watercourses, once blue ribbons of the sky laid on the rosy mauve of the broad flagged pathways, now look meaningless and forlorn. The majority of the Mughal gardens are on such a huge scale that it seems, at first sight, almost vain to hope for their complete restoration. But the tomb of I'timad-ud-Daulah and its enclosure are comparatively small, and it is easy to realise how much this exquisite mausoleum would gain in beauty and interest if its old setting were revived. The delicious flash and sparkle of the water running through its narrow channels would give life and character to the broad stone-ways and platforms; the deep gloom of the cypress avenues, a welcome relief and perspective, changing the glare of sunshine on white inlaid marble to a soft iridescent bloom. Rose-bushes should border the raised walks, bending over to break the hard edges of the stone-work, and drop their petals in tribute at the tomb of this Persian scholar and rose-lover. On the grass plots by the river brilliant parterres might be spread, with fruit trees planted formally, for without their changing beauties of fruit and blossom no Moslem or Hindu garden is complete.

This is a tempting subject on which to enlarge, for apart from the symbolic appropriateness, the mere artistic gain would be great if this garden by the riverside at Agra could be replanted with the same care, skill, and knowledge with which its buildings have been restored.

The small scale of this garden shows the old symbolism of the plan very clearly. The central building on its platform, the four springs,—in this case four tanks on each side of the platform itself, each containing a single fountain,—and the four watercourses, " the Rivers of Life," which they supply.

The first time I saw this simple and oldest of all garden-plans, I was vividly reminded of our own early struggles to lay out a garden in the Central Province station whither my husband's military work had temporarily transplanted us. New to India, I had only seen the English villa gardens of Bombay, green certainly, but feature-

PLATE IX.

FLORAL DETAIL FROM THE TAJ DADO.

less, uninteresting, and quite unlike the Indian gardens of my dreams. With us, fortunately, water was plentiful, so our first idea was to build as large a fountain as might be, and a central tank from which to irrigate the garden. The space was small, but gradually the natural plan unfolded itself, the long flower-bordered walks leading from the central tank; though I remember how I argued at great length against the mali's (gardener) insistance that the walks should be raised above the garden level, unconsciously clinging, in my own mind, to the opposite English plan of the flat paths with their raised herbaceous borders. The mali won the day, though I was slow, I confess, to see the obvious fact that the walks, in an irrigated garden, must be necessarily raised for the water to pass under them. It was astonishing how quickly and willingly the work was done; quite large cypress trees were planted, and the whole garden, previously a burnt-up field, soon took shape. When it was planted I was quite unaware of its propitious symbolism, how even the "good" snake was not wanting, a cobra which lived curled up in the roots of the old mango tree at the end of one of the four walks. How horrified I should have been had I known that at the time. But a year later when I discovered the fact, it seemed only fitting; and Naga, the friendly deity, was left undisturbed in the enjoyment of his daily offering of milk, wherefore our garden prospered, and, in evil times, our compound proved free from plague!

CHAPTER III

THE GARDENS OF THE TAJ

I sometimes think that never blows so red
The Rose as where some buried Caesar bled;
That every Hyacinth the Garden wears,
Dropt in her Lap from some once lovely Head.

OMAR KHAYYÁM.

THE "Paradise-like Orchard" of the Lady Arjumand Banu, Begam, is more familiar to us as the garden-tomb of Mumtaz Mahal—the Crown of the Palace and Lady of the Taj.

So much has been written in praise of this famous building, and photographs and pictures have made it so familiar, that it might seem needless to add any impressions of my own, were it not that most writers are too enchanted with the beauty of the actual tomb to realise the close connection of the whole group of buildings, and that the garden as originally planned formed an integral part of one great design.

An early visit to the Taj stands out vividly in my mind: the bitter cold of the drive in the half-light of an Indian November morning; a stray jackal flitting across the wide road, like the embodiment of some "devil-spirit" escaping before the grey disillusioning dawn; the chill of the rising mists mingling with the acrid smoke of the little fires of twigs and fallen leaves over which the road sweepers crouched. The shops in the alcoves beside the great doorway of the caravansarai were securely boarded up; no shrill voices greeted me in noisy rivalry, demanding attention to the charms of picture post-cards or their owners' wasted skill in carving toy marble tombs. The great square within at this early hour lay peaceful and empty. Presently at the entrance to the gardens appeared the aged door-keeper, unmistakably cross at being roused at such an hour. All day long the restless white-faced tourists came; on moonlight nights the gardens were often full of sightseers; but a man must have his rest, and it was clear he did not hold with foolish folk who might wish to see the gardens at sunrise.

The light increased rapidly as I hurried up

PLATE X.

"THE GATES WERE AS OF PEARL."

the flights of steps and under the splendid arch, over which, inlaid in black marble, the flowing Arabic letters invite the pure of heart to enter the Gardens of Paradise. Seen from within the entrance portal, rising above the mists which wrapped the cypress trees and blurred the reflections in the wide canal, the Taj itself loomed white and ghostly—cheerless against a pale grey sky. Then, as I reached the water's edge, with a flash the topmost golden iris of the spire took the sun. Softly and rapidly the rosy light stole round the exquisite curve of the dome, flushing the smooth, pearly surface of the marble, till, striking the sides of the building, the sunshine at length reached the great white platform, lighting up each arched recess in a marvel of mauve shade and amber reflection; a fairy beauty, a spirit building, "whose gates were as of pearl," hovering for a moment over earth. With the warmth of the sunrise the garden mists rose high, drifting away in turquoise wreaths between the deep green of the guardian cypress trees; whose slender shapes and curving topmost crests were now clearly mirrored in the still water, while between their dark reflections shone the Taj, a miracle revealed.

The magic lasted but a moment, but in that moment I had seen the vision as its builders saw and planned it long ago—the vision which Mr. Havell with so much insight describes when he says: "Those critics who have objected to the effeminacy of the architecture unconsciously pay the highest tribute to the genius of the builders. The Taj was meant to be feminine. The whole conception, and every line and detail of it express the intention of the designers. It is Mumtaz Mahal herself, radiant in her youthful beauty, who still lingers on the banks of the shining Jumna, at early morn, in the glowing midday sun, or in the silver moonlight. Or rather, we should say, it conveys a more abstract thought; it is India's noble tribute to the grace of Indian womanhood—the Venus de Milo of the East."

As the sunlight flooded the gardens, the avenue of cypresses stood out sharply, their shadows barring the long walks. But the dark masses of the mango trees behind looked confused and heavy, blocking the full view of the magnificent platform with the white marble mausoleum and its attendant mosques. The noise of a flock of chattering, shrieking parrots rose behind me as the garden coolies, and the sweepers with their brooms, and the bhistis with their water mussicks all clattered noisily through the echoing entrance portal; and in a somewhat dilatory fashion, with much talk and shouting, the day's work of the garden began.

The Taj is the one triumph of Indian art in which Moslem and Hindu, official Anglo-Indian and passing English tourist all join to reverence and admire. And in the full prosaic daylight, when the white dome stands up in dazzling sharpness against the deep blue of the sky, nothing is more striking, in a land of great ruins and tawdry modern buildings, than its absolute bloom of perfection.

The earliest existing plan of the gardens is that made in 1828 by Colonel Hodgson, Surveyor-General in India, from which it will be seen that beautifully kept as they are at present, the grounds have been considerably Europeanised, and cannot now be said to represent the original intention of their makers. For one thing, the heavy mass of trees quite obscures the view of the composition as a whole. The plan is simple: the fourfold field-plot of Babar, the plan of Arama, the ancient Hindu fourfold

Paradise of restfulness. In one particular only does the plan of the Taj differ from those of all

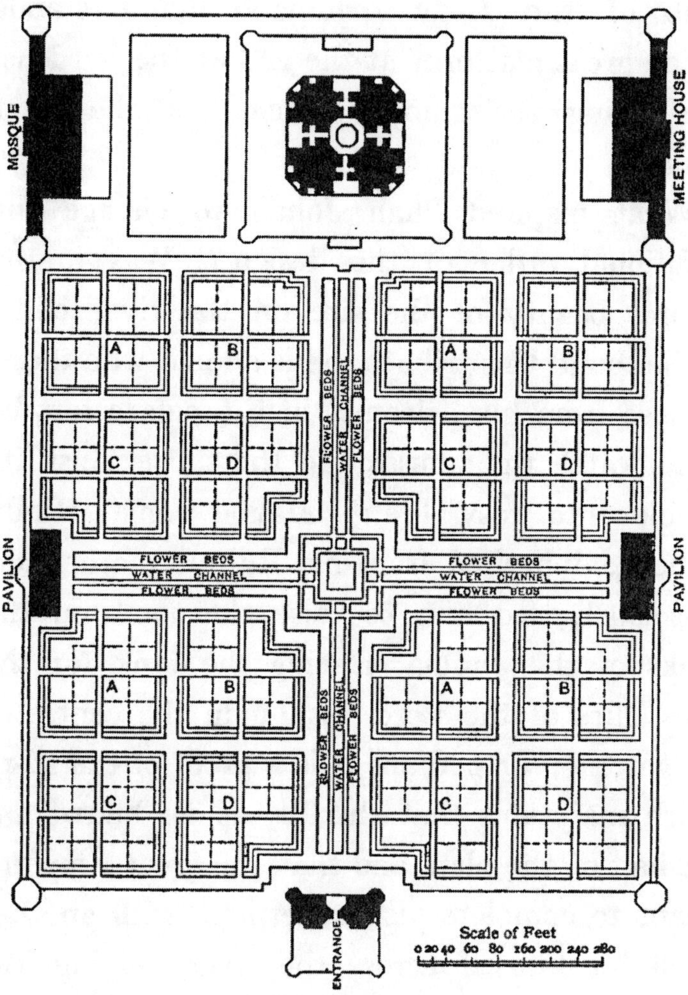

TAJ GARDEN.

(Colonel Hodgson's Plan.)

other famous Mughal tombs. A beautiful raised fountain-tank of white marble occupies the centre of the fourfold plot, replacing the almost invariable central mausoleum; and the actual tomb of the Lady Arjumand Banu stands on the great platform at the end of the gardens, overlooking the shining reaches of the river Jumna.

What inspired Shah Jahan to change the traditional order of the design? Was it the natural beauty of the site on the river cliff? Did he build this tribute to his adored wife there, because from his balconies in the palace fort he could watch the sunrise and the sunset flush its marble into rosy life? Maybe some Hindu influence, inherited from his Rajput mother unconsciously, led him to raise the tomb on the banks of the Jumna, placing the tank for the lotus lilies of the Lord Vishnu in the centre of the garden; or perhaps it is a proof of the story which maintains that the Taj as we know it is but half of the plan, and that the great Emperor meant to complete his masterpiece with another tomb for himself across the river, joining Taj to Taj by a bridge of black marble—Holy Jumna itself the centre of the scheme.

Bernier gives an account of the gardens as he saw them in about 1660. Looking over the grounds from the high platform of the mausoleum, he says: "To the left and right of that dome on the lower surface you observe several garden walks covered with trees and many parterres of flowers. . . . Between the end of the principal walk and this dome is an open and pretty large space, which I call a water parterre, because the stones on which you walk, cut and figured in various forms, represent the borders of box in our parterres." Here it would seem that Bernier is describing the great platform of the Taj itself. Although he is, as a rule, singularly clear and accurate in his observations and statements, in his account of his visit to "the Paradise of the Indies" (Kashmir) with the Emperor Aurungzeb he speaks of sailing up the whole length of the Shalimar Bagh, but as this garden is on three distinct levels, it is a little difficult to understand how he accomplished the feat. Be that as it may, in spite of his natural preference for all things French, this genial old Parisian cannot restrain his admiration for the Mughal buildings, even though he finds "the columns, the architraves and cornices are, indeed, not formed according to the proportion of the five orders of architecture so strictly observed in French edifices." When, as in 1660, a splendid living art flourished in Europe, that of India was not despised. And I cannot leave Bernier at the Taj without quoting the following delightful extract: "The last time I visited Tage Mehale's mausoleum I was in company of a French merchant, who, as well as myself, thought that this extraordinary fabric could not be sufficiently admired. I did not venture to express my opinion, fearing that my taste might have become corrupted by my long residence in the Indies; and as my companion was come recently from France, it was quite a relief to my mind to hear him say that he had seen nothing in Europe so bold and majestic."

The various gay parterres mentioned by Bernier have all been swept away, excepting only the stone-bordered, star-shaped beds along the canals, which are now laid out in grass. The cypress avenues have been replanted, but one looks round the garden in vain for that favourite motive which so many forms of Moslem art borrowed from garden-craft, the symbolic mixed avenues of cypress and flowering tree. Palms have recently been planted round the central raised tank and its fountain parterre.

At present they look heavy and stumpy, but in the future, when they tower with their graceful heads above the cypress trees, they will mark the centre of the gardens, without obstructing the view of the monument; their slender stems repeating the idea of the graceful detached minarets at the four corners of the Taj platform. And in this famous Indian garden these four areca-nut palms opposite the four corners of the tank would combine this artistic purpose with the old Hindu symbolism of the marriage of the fruit trees—one of which was usually a palm—by the well.

Jahangir, in his Memoirs, mentions an avenue of areca-nut palms in one of Babar's gardens at Agra which had grown ninety feet high. The gardens of Akbar's tomb at Sikandrah were planted with cypress, wild-pine, plane, and supari (areca-nut palm). Another garden made by Jahangir's directions at Sehrind he describes thus: "On entering the garden I found myself immediately in a covered avenue (pergola), planted on each side with scarlet roses, and beyond them arose groves of cypress, fir, plane, and evergreens variously disposed. . . . Passing through these we entered what was in reality the garden, which now exhibited a variegated parterre ornamented with flowers of the utmost brilliancy of colours and of the choicest kinds."

Akbar (1556–1605) was keenly interested in horticulture, though garden building and design do not seem to have had for him the attraction they had for his grandfather Babar or his son Jahangir. The Ain-i-Akbari gives in detail the principal plants and flowers of the time. "His Majesty looks upon plants as one of the greatest gifts of the Creator, and pays much attention to them. The horticulturists of Iran and Turan have, therefore, settled here, and the cultivation of the trees is in a flourishing state."

In Babar's garden at Agra, named by him the "Flower Scatterer," thousands of pine-apples were produced yearly. One wonders if the red-flowered oleanders flourished there, "the particularly fine red kanirs" which Babar found in a garden at Gwalior and transplanted with such care to his new gardens at Agra.

In speaking of gardens Jahangir refers to those of the nobles of his Court, remains of which can still be seen on the bank of the Jumna at Agra. He stayed, he tells us, in the Dil Amiz Garden at Lahore. He specially remarks on the gardens of Kabul; the City Adorning Garden, with a stream eight feet wide running down its centre, which he and his courtiers tried to jump but failed. He says on this day he walked round seven of the famous gardens of Kabul, and adds, "I do not think I ever walked so far before.

"First of all I walked round the City Adorning, then the Moonlight Garden, then the garden that Bika Begam, grandmother of my father, had made, then passed through the Middle Garden, then a garden that Maryam-makani, my own grandmother, had prepared, then the Surat-khana garden, which has a large chenar tree, the like of which there is not in the other gardens of Kabul. Then having seen the Char-Bagh, which is the largest of the City gardens, I returned to my own abode. There were abundance of cherries on the trees, each of which looked as it were a round ruby hanging like globes on the branches. The Shahr-ara Bagh was made by Shahr-Banu Begam, daughter of Mirza Abu Said, who was own aunt to the late king Babar. From time to time it has been added to, and there is not a garden like it for sweetness in Kabul. It has all sorts of fruits and grapes and its softness is such that to put one's sandalled feet on it would be far from propriety or good manners. In the neighbourhood of this garden an excellent plot of land came to view which I ordered to be bought from the owners. I ordered a stream that flows from the Guzargah to be diverted into the middle of the ground so that a garden might be made such that in beauty and sweetness there should not be in the inhabited world another like it. I gave it the name of 'World Adorning.' Whilst I was at Kabul I had several entertainments in the City Adorning Garden, sometimes with my intimates and courtiers, sometimes with the ladies of the harem."

On his visits to various towns the Emperor Jahangir speaks of having planned and built several other gardens. He saw one garden with one hundred mango trees and a huge banyan in it which especially called for remark. On another occasion he had a "nice feast" in the Nagina Bagh, "where a pergola of grapes had ripened." At Ahmedabad he went to a little garden "which had exceedingly good figs," and while there he visited the Fath Bagh (Garden of Victory) and contemplated the red roses. "The plot," he said, "had bloomed well, it was pleasant to see so many there owing to their scarcity in India." "The anemone bed, too, was not bad, and the figs had ripened." In yet another garden at Ahmedabad he particularises "orange, lemon, peach, pomegranate, and apple trees, and among flowering shrubs every kind of rose."

Flowering shrubs and some roses still adorn the Taj gardens; but where are the fruit trees? The orange, pomegranate, and lemon? Groves of these should certainly be again planted here, for quite apart from their great decorative value, they formed a special feature of the original design and pious intentions of the founder of this Paradise Orchard. Undoubtedly the different squares of the garden were largely planted with fruit trees, while, to relieve the monotony, the corners marked A B C D on the plan were most probably treated as parterres.

For a month, every sunrise and sunset found me in these gardens; and among all the sunny days one grey day stands out alone.

It had been raining, a sudden sharp burst of the early winter rains. The water stood in great pools along the worn stone pathways, extending the reflections of the wide canal and brimming over the edges of the fountain parterre round the central tank. A soft grey bloom of raindrops veiled the grass and clung to the tapering cypress spires, while beyond them, against a background of purple cloud, the Taj, more exquisite than ever, seemed sharply carved in mellow ivory; smooth, solid ivory of every tone from palest cream to a soft, deep ochre, where the rain had stained the marble. A long-forgotten first sight of Pisa in winter flashed back on my mind as I gazed entranced at this strange new Taj, with its quiet harmonies of grey-green, and cream, and purple.

Up on the high platform of the mausoleum, the moisture glistened on the waving black and white lines of the inlaid pavement, whose symbolic ripples carry out an old Indian tradition, so that the Taj, like many an ancient Hindu shrine, stands in the centre of a tank. Here, on most days, the glare of sunshine radiating up from this dazzling pavement is quite blinding, and all but obscures the lovely details of the dado round the building; but in the more subdued light the inlaid borders and delicate carving of the floral panels showed clearly. This dado is one of the most charming examples of Mughal decorative work, and like the parterres which it naïvely represents—for the design is taken directly from the oblong flower-beds, such as were seen beside the canals of every palace garden—it only reveals its full delicacy of form and colour on a dull day. How delicious they are, these formal flower-beds, with their blue-bells, daffodils, tulips, crown-imperials, lilies, and irises, which stand up swaying on their slender stems by the black and white marble ripples, forming a fairy circle round the tomb. Spring flowers all of them, for the Rose of Persia and the Lotus of the Good Law hold a truce, and are missing from this gathering of the flowers. Maybe the famous Kashmir gardens of the Empress Nur Jahan were the artist's inspiration here. In the record, which is still preserved, of the craftsmen employed on the Taj, the name appears of one Ram Lal Kashmiri, proving that at least one Kashmir artist was employed by Shah Jahan.

Great was my delight, some months after this rainy day at Agra, to forget the fatigue of the long three days' drive up the Jhelum ravine, as I found one by one the spring flowers of the Taj. First came the tulips, high up on the slopes of the Murree Hills, growing in little patches where the sun could reach them through the fir trees, dainty little cream-coloured flowers, with pointed petals streaked on the outer sides with carmine. Lower, the hillsides were bare as yet, but down in the ravine by the river the lilies were coming out, in form like our Madonna lilies, but smaller, pink in colour, with long reed-like leaves, growing in tufts in crevices of the limestone cliffs, tantalisingly out of reach. Then as the rocks receded and the valley grew more wooded, splendid crown-imperials shot up through the mossy carpet strewn with the brown of last year's leaves, magnificent great red bells, which glowed between the bare mauve twigs and russet buds of the undergrowth. Each flower as we passed it I thought the loveliest of all, but the craftsman who crowned the crescent of the Taj with an iris knew best, for the memory of the other lilies fades before the blue Kashmir iris as we saw it when at last the valley opened out: blue lakes and pools of iris, between a golden land of mustard fields and reefs of bright green grass, stretching away into the gloomy deep-blue distance of the lower mountain chains, above which towered the cloud-wreathed summits of the snowy Pir Panjal.

Most of these blossoms reappear inlaid on the actual tombs of Mumtaz Mahal and Shah Jahan, and they decorate the famous screen which surrounds the graves. This screen, the flower dado, and the Sultana's bath in the Jasmine Tower of the fort, exhibit to perfection that marvellous decorative feeling which seems inborn in Oriental craftsmen. Each is a masterpiece in its combination of inlaid jewelled colour and delicate marble carving. It is impossible to decide which is the most faultless: the screen, seen in the dim light under the dome, with its lattice-work of lilies and its upper rail, whereon a row of marble vases blooming with never-fading flowers stand round the shrine; the marble flower-beds without; or the fountain-bath of the Jasmine Tower. Where the four shallow curves of the fountain basin are carved with the flow of the water, the vivid red and green of the inlaid flowers and leaves shine through the ripples like the pebbles of the wet sea-beach, and the white marble lily-buds seem to float away, dragged down by the swirl of the stream.

To realise even faintly Shah Jahan's dream, it is necessary to go over to the other side of the Jumna. A crazy ferry-boat plies between the sand-banks, winding slowly in and out with the current, carrying from time to time little groups of country people across the stream. Few other craft are seen on the river. But day by day, as I made up my mind to attempt the expedition and looked over the low parapet of the Taj platform for the ferry-boat, it always seemed hopelessly stranded on some far-off bank. At last, one afternoon, just as the boatman was leisurely pushing off, I caught it, and, much to the astonishment of the other passengers, demanded to be taken across. The boat was a wretched old affair, leaking everywhere, and the three dry planks on which we all crouched seemed little protection between us and an ominous dark snout and trailing oily streak, that showed where the ever hungry Mugger of the ford haunted these waters. On the far side a red sandstone tower and long ruined wall marked the site of what once had been a garden—perhaps originally one of the regular and elegant gardens built by Yunis Ali or some other faithful friend of Babar, those cheery friends of his Memoirs, lightly sketched with such seemingly artless skill. Hassein Beg, the good-humoured man, "of plain simple manners," who "excelled in singing at drinking parties." Kamber Ali Mughal, who could not stand prosperity, but "after he had gained a certain elevation he became negligent and perverse. He talked a good deal and very idly; indeed, there can be no doubt that a great talker must often talk foolishly. He was a man of narrow capacity and muddy brain."

Of uncertain date, this building by the banks of the Jumna had long since fallen into decay. Thorn bushes stopped my passage along the wall which had once been the rampart of the now vanished garden; and the level cultivated land stretched away to the horizon, broken only where the clumps of trees marked the villages. Looking back, the sight of the great pile of buildings on the far side of the river was worth all the trouble of crossing it. For the first time I had a full view of the whole group, and realised the great scale on which it had been conceived; the vast walls and platforms rising sheer above the water, the two great rose-red mosques, the corner towers, with their elaborate arcades, and, raised on the central platform high above all, the pale lilac minarets, walls, and dome of the Taj worked in shadow, and outlined with the gold thread of the western sun, while below, reflected in the slow-flowing tranquil Jumna, shone another Taj—the second Taj of Shah Jahan's unrealised ideal.

Coming in under the deep shadow of the high river walls, their bold panels, filled with vases of flowers cut in the hard red sandstone, surprise one with ever fresh delight, so striking is the wonderful finish yet perfect subordination of all parts to the whole design,—even each battlement of the garden wall has its star of white marble inlay,—and walking back up the broad landing-ghat paved with brick-work in various patterns, one sees the Taj as no doubt Bernier and Tavernier first saw it when they sailed down stream, leaving the Court of Aurungzeb in the fort to visit this famous tomb.

As one stands on the river terrace at evening, Babar's disgust with the country round Agra hardly seems justified. But then what Babar looked for was a hillside spring around which he could construct a great terraced garden like those of Samarkand, and such as he built himself at Kabul; and, at first, in his search for a good site he evidently overlooked the advantages offered by the width and steep bank of the Jumna, a river so different from the rushing torrents of his own northern mountains.

Choice of site, and the genius of the place, are the first considerations of a garden-maker everywhere. Nowhere are they more essential than in the case of an Indian garden, where the success of the great enclosure depends largely on the lie of the land enabling the builder to substitute a terrace and retaining wall for one of the four high encircling ramparts. This change of plan gives to the garden that double charm of complete seclusion and a wide prospect over the world without the walls.

A steep mountain-side offers one fine opportunity, the bank of a broad river another.

The Nishat Bagh in Kashmir and the Taj gardens at Agra are each perfect of their kind: one a stately terraced hillside garden, the other a gracious riverside garden of the plains.

From the high embankment of the Taj, where on either hand octagonal towers jut out conspicuously over the stream, the view of the river is very fine. Octagonal buildings, called chattris or baradaris, mark the angles of the walls in all old Indian gardens. Delightful little summer-houses they are, in which to sit and revel in the distant view; and in the contrast of the burnt-up arid land outside the garden's boundary with the misty fountains, glistening leaves, and vivid colours of the fruit and flowers within. Along the banks of the Jumna many of these old towers still mark the sites of ruined gardens. The octagonal baradaris of the Taj are large and elaborate buildings rising up in five stories from the water's edge. Towards sunset, looking back on Agra city and fort, one of these towers is silhouetted against the sky, all its white marble details lost in the warm dusk of the sandstone, forming a dark foreground to the distant view; the bold turn of the river where the palms of a long deserted garden lean over the silver-grey sand-banks, in and out of which, sweeping in great curves, the river finds its way and swings across to where it flows under the old fortress walls. The towers, and high white buildings of the city, lie almost lost beneath the gathering films of mist and smoke, save for one slender spire, which tells of wise, tolerant days when the great Akbar granted leave and land for every teacher, and India all but turned to meet the Christian claim. Nearer, the fort stands up, a dark mass of solid masonry, against which the

PLATE XI.

THE SULTANA'S FOUNTAIN BATH. (JASMINE TOWER.)

Jasmine Tower glimmers faintly, showing the arches through which Shah Jahan last saw the vision of his love; and crowning the citadel, floating like bubbles in the evening air, shine the three pearly domes of the royal mosque.

CHAPTER IV

THE AGRA GRAPE GARDEN

But still a Ruby kindles in the Vine,
And many a Garden by the Water blows.

OMAR KHAYYÁM.

THE royal palace within the fort at Agra, like every other Indian house or palace, once contained several open squares laid out in gardens. " All these palaces (Delhi, Agra, Lahore) are full of gardens with running water, which flows in channels into reservoirs of stone, jasper, and marble. In all the rooms and halls of these palaces there are ordinarily fountains or reservoirs of the same stone and of proportionate size. In the gardens of these palaces there are always flowers according to the season. There are no large fruit trees of any sort, in order not to hinder the delight of an open view. In these palaces are seats and private rooms, some of which are in the midst of running water. In the water are many fish for delight." This description of Niccolao Manucci's, in his *Storia do Mogor*, gives a vivid impression of what the Machchi Bhawan (the Fish Square) and the Anguri Bagh, two of the principal squares in the palace at Agra, looked like before their spoliation. Now, alas! what between the Jats of Bharatpur, who carried off the marble fountains and tanks to the palace of Suraj Mal at Deeg, and Lord William Bentinck, who sold what was left of the mosaic and marble fret-work, there is nothing left in the garden of the sacred fish from which to realise its former magnificence.

The Anguri Bagh has fared better. This garden lies in front of the Khas Mahal and is enclosed on three sides by arcades. It was the principal square of the zenana apartments, and is a typical specimen of an old Mughal garden, laid out in geometrical stone-edged parterres, with four terraced walks radiating from a central chabutra, with a raised fountain tank. A stone trellis formerly enclosed the flower-beds, and is thought by some to have supported vines, but the name of Anguri Bagh (Grape Garden) was more probably derived from the vine pattern decoration in precious stones which Shah Jahan constructed

PLATE XII.

THE RIVER TERRACE OF THE TAJ.

at enormous cost in the corner near the Jasmine Tower.

Through all the troublous times, in which the fort has been besieged, taken and retaken, looted by the Jats, turned into a barracks by the English, this zenana quarter of the palace seems to have been more or less respected; and an indefinable charm still pervades these buildings and lingers in the cool green shadows of their arches. Viewed from the open garden square, these palace rooms form a wonderful group; all are still perfect, save only for an ugly modern marble rail which catches the eye, disfiguring and stunting the proportions of the upper story of the Jasmine Tower.

Among the many improvements that were made by Lord Curzon in the fort was the clearance of the wire-netting fern houses and bedraggled shrubs which at one time disfigured the Anguri Bagh.

Wherever one wanders throughout India, the name of Lord Curzon rises up in connection with some fine work of restoration—a sort of beneficent djinn, whose good deeds lose nothing in the telling. Everywhere from guardians of the ancient gates the same tale meets the ear:

"In the days of Curzon Lat-Sahib it was done"; "Behold, Huzoor, the Great Lat-Sahib commanded, and it rose again from the ground"; and Indians and Englishmen alike owe him a great debt of gratitude for his timely rescue of many magnificent old Indian buildings and works of art. It is little short of marvellous, even for the East, to find how one man has inspired and accomplished so much good work in so short a time. It is not to be wondered at that his work stopped short at archæology; and that though the Mughal gardens were cleared of much accumulated overgrowth and rubbish, there has been so far no serious attempt to revive the old garden-craft in its artistic and symbolic aspects.

The whole effect of the palace square at Agra suffers sadly from the loss of its flowers and fountain jets; as can be realised on comparing the two illustrations, one of the beautiful but empty Anguri Bagh, all its straight lines left exposed in hard monotony, and the illustration taken from an old Indian painting of an evening scene in a Rajputana garden. The latter shows a typically planted palace square. The four dark cypress spires planted at angles of the paths round the little central pavilion, delightfully repeat the lines of the four slender pillars, the feathery heads of the palms tower high above the outer walls, the walks are bordered by sweet-scented tuberoses and hollyhocks planted alternately, and in front, close to the little fountain, a bed of poppies makes a solid mass of colour, softening the harsh edge of the white marble platform with their frail, transparent flowers.

From old Indian miniature paintings such as this, some idea can be gathered of the planting of these Paradise gardens, whose beauty formed the chief symbolic and artistic inspiration of Mughal decorative art.

This idea of Paradise underlay the whole artistic world of the Mughal craftsman, builder, and artist. It included the angels, and houris, the gentle beasts, and bright birds, and glittering fishes whose home it was, and who all lived together there in perfect harmony; for although the stricter conventions of some Moslem sects might forbid their representation, no idea of an Indian Paradise garden is complete without their presence, as well as the more familiar forms of trees, and fruits, and flowers, and running waters. Whatever building or smaller work of art we turn to, the same garden motives reappear: in the beautiful inlaid flower-bed dados of the Private Hall of Audience beyond the Anguri Bagh, in the similar dado round the Taj, in the well-known rose-water vessels and flower-vases, the fruit-plates and wine-cups of the old Persian and Indian tiles, they are equally to be found. Bouquets of flowers cover the fine gold-embroidered muslins; flower-borders edge the soft Kashmir shawls, and twine lightly in and out of the pages of much-prized Nasta'liq writing. The miniature portraits of Emperors, and their nobles, often show a garden background; and in nearly every case the figure holds in one hand a sweet-scented garden flower, some rose or narcissus painted with precise, delicious skill. The waving pattern of the water is seen on every hand; pavements and platforms are inlaid to represent the garden tanks; the same motive echoes the charm of the waterfalls on embroidered rugs and hangings. The best known and most beautiful theme of all, the entwined cypress and fruit tree, which appears and reappears on carpets, in tiles, embroideries, and paintings, was taken directly from the garden avenues, where cypress and fruit trees planted

PLATE XIII.

THE ANGURI BAGH.

alternately were the favourite symbols of life, death, and eternity; the solemn background of the deep-toned cypress, emblem of death and eternity, contrasted with the waving, delicate sprays of rosy almond tree or silvery flowering plum, emblems of life and hope.

The designs of the old Firdus (Paradise) carpets were, as their name implies, directly taken from some such garden parterre as those which still exist in outline in the Anguri Bagh; where each of the four squares which make up the whole design has its separate border and central plot, once, like the carpets, full of brightly-coloured flowers woven into a close geometrical pattern. The Mughal parterres must not be confused with the English "carpet bedding" of mid-Victorian days—tiny coloured leaves and flowers worked into a tedious pattern along some border or bank—but were boldly massed flowers of varying heights and beautifully chosen colours, like the lily beds of the Taj dados, the red rose garden of Jahangir's Memoirs, the narcissus, anemone, and tulip plots that so delighted Babar. The surrounding border was treated differently in oblong beds of alternate colouring, or else with single flowers like the groups of hollyhock and tuberoses. The customary mixed avenues of trees were only for larger gardens, but in palace squares, like that of Anguri Bagh, a cypress tree planted in the border nearly always marked the angles of the design, while the centre of each plot was sometimes occupied by a fruit tree or a palm.

The replanting of the Anguri Bagh might prove difficult chiefly on account of the need for providing an adequate water-supply so high up in the fort. But would it not be worth doing if it helped to revive the dying art of Indian gardening ? Are the wonderful surroundings of this square, so full of beauty and historic interest, not worth completing by the restoration of the garden ? As a living example of Mughal art at its best, it would mean more, educationally and artistically, than all the priceless Mughal treasures locked away, isolated, in many fine but lifeless museums. What would the present archæologists and artists of France and Italy not give to have this perfect setting of the Anguri Bagh for their labours ? Now, when so much is done to revive old conditions, when the columns of the Roman forum and the ruins of Pompeiian villas are restored so carefully and artistically, that even the shrubs and trees that grew beside them in past times have been replanted, as in the garden of the Vestal Virgins, or the Villa of the Vettii.

The Anguri Bagh in the Agra fort is the one garden in the three great Mughal palaces left complete with its old stone and marble details; and yet there it lies, bare and empty, with only grass between its masonry, like some great, elaborate, jewelled design rifled of its coloured gems, turning its gaping empty setting to the sun.

CHAPTER V

GARDENS OF THE PLAINS—DELHI

If there is a Paradise on Earth, it is Here, it is Here.

SADI.

Not only the Nightingale in the Rose-bushes sings his hymn
of praise,
But every Thorn is itself a voice of adoration to the Deity.

SADI.

A STRANGE fascination, the very spirit of the age-long capital of India, hovers over the wide, rolling campagna, the sandy fields and thorny scrub, the gaunt brown domes of ruined tombs, the half-submerged mosques, forts, and palaces, which lie between the Jumna river-bed and the red sunbaked rocks of the famous Ridge which runs from Ajmeer northward until it dies away beyond the plains of Delhi.

No other capital can boast of so long continued a history beginning with King Yudisthara, the central hero of the Mahabharata, whose city, now known as Purana Kila (the Old Fort),

PLATE XIV.

Calcutta School of Art.

A RAJPUTANA GARDEN.

marks the south-western angle of the capital of the English-Aryan King-Emperor of India.

Six Delhis lie between Purana Kila and the Ridge; six capitals of Empires each famous in its day; but the plain has conquered all save one: the vast, relentless, sandy plain, broken only where the Kutb Tower of Victory soars up against the sky, the grim dark walls of Tughlakabad rise deserted but defiant, or the fairy gates of Indraspat catch the sunset light on the site of Yudisthara's legendary citadel.

Shah Jahanabad, modern Delhi as we call it, still stands, and a wonderful city it is. A palace, fort, and city built at one time, by one man, and that man an Emperor, an artist, and the greatest builder of his day. Fergusson, in his *Indian Architecture*, says that the whole conception of the palace-fort, with its entrance built to look straight down the Chandi Chauk (the Moonlight Market), with its trees and long canal full of running water, forms the finest approach to "the most magnificent palace in the East—perhaps in the world." Near the fort, too, stands the grand Jama Masjid, the cathedral mosque of India, yet with all these magnificent buildings the strangest thing about this wonderful city is the fact that it cannot long claim our sole interest: the plains triumph even here, for Shah Jahanabad is only one of many Delhis.

The garden-tomb of Humayun, the first Mughal Emperor buried in India, lies south of Shah Jahanabad on the plains near the river, between the Emperor's own fort of Purana Kila and the older Delhi of Tughlak Shah. Babar was buried in his favourite Garden of the New Year near Kabul, but his son and successor Humayun, whom he died to save, rests outside the capital of the New Mughal Empire.

The story of Babar's death is told by the historian Adul-Fazl, Akbar's confidant and greatest friend. Humayun, Babar's only son by his wife Mahum, of whom he was so fond, had been away from Agra and was brought back dying of fever. Nothing apparently could be done, and the doctors, powerless, gave up all hope. The mercy of God alone could save him now, they declared. Some supreme sacrifice might avail.

The Emperor, to whom this was suggested, caught eagerly at the hope. He would sacrifice his own life. In vain the Koh-i-nor was suggested instead—the great diamond given up at

PLATE XV.

THE FEAST OF THE BIRTH OF HUMAYUN.

the taking of Gwalior from the Rajputs. But that splendid offering to God was rejected. Babar would have none of it: "The dearest thing I have is my life, and that is the dearest thing on earth to my son." Persisting in his resolution, he walked, according to the solemn sacrificial usage, three times round his son's bed, praying earnestly. Suddenly he was heard to exclaim: "I have borne it away! I have borne it away!" From this moment, Mussulman historians assert, Humayun began to recover, while Babar slowly sank: his health impaired with his forty-eight years of strenuous activities and ceaseless hardships, and now fatally undermined by anxiety and nervous prostration. So passed away the Emperor Babar, on the 26th of December 1530, after thirty-six years of kingship.

Pilgrims still visit his grave at Kabul, the grave of the first of the great Mughals. Well they may, for there lies the most romantic, gallant, genial Prince of Oriental history. "Heaven is the eternal abode of the Emperor Babar," they wrote on his tomb; but his epitaph can best be written in his own words—those in which he describes his father in his Memoirs:—"His generosity was large, and so was his whole soul, yet brave withal and manly."

Few of us can follow the pilgrims to the Garden of the New Year, but most of us in India visit Agra. Every Englishman who does so should lay a tribute at Sikandrah on the grave of the great Peacemaker and Statesman, Akbar, who had the gift which wins all hearts, and should not forget to scatter there a few sweet-scented flowers in memory of Babar, from whom his grandson inherited that precious talisman.

Humayun's actual reign was short and troubled, but he must be remembered here for three things: he was the father of the great Akbar—the baby son born to him and his sixteen-year old bride in their flight across the Sind Desert; his capital during the few years of his reign in India was the Purana Kila, the most beautiful fort of the many ruined Delhis; and the tomb, raised to his memory by his childless first wife, was the first great architectural monument of the Mughals, the plan of which was adopted eighty years after for the Taj.

The mausoleum is about four miles to the south of modern Delhi; the road to it branching off from the main highway runs past the fine tomb of Isa Khan, and round the corner of an old garden wall with picturesque, brightly-tiled baradaris. The great dome of Humayun's tomb is the most conspicuous building in all the plains around Delhi; but the garden, a square of thirteen acres, in the midst of which the mausoleum stands, looks bare and disappointing. Its interest, however, lies in the fact that it is the earliest Mughal garden in India which still preserves intact its original plan. The Ram Bagh, at Agra, is of course earlier, but there the design is quite obscured by modern roads and plantations. At Humayun's garden-tomb, on the other hand, the stone channels and fountain basins have lately been carefully restored; though unhappily the garden seems to have been swept bare of its characteristic fruit trees and shade.

The site chosen for this Mughal garden of the plains is practically level, and like the Taj the garden ends in a terrace on the old river-bank. The invariable watercourse, with raised paths on either hand, leads up from the gateway to the mausoleum, but the water channel is very narrow, being hardly two feet across. Instead of the usual simple plan—the four long waterways—the garden is made up of a labyrinth of little channels. These form an inner and an outer square enclosing the high platform of the tomb, ornamented, wherever the paths cross each other, with a small tank, sometimes on the same level, sometimes sunk in the centre of a raised chabutra. The numerous little tanks are outwardly square, with a lower inside ledge of stone, modifying them into oval, octagonal, or round water basins, the whole effect being reminiscent of the shallow fountains and narrow watercourses of the earliest gardens in Kashmir. The illustration, Plate XV. from the copy of Babar's Memoirs, gives a picture of the feast of the birth of Humayun, which takes place in just such a garden.

After his son's birth, Babar, who was at Kabul at the time, and had newly styled himself Badshah (Emperor), went, as was customary on such occasions, to the Char Bagh outside the city for four or five days to celebrate the festival of Humayun's nativity. "Those who were Begs, and those who were not," he writes, "great and small, brought their offerings. Bags of silver money were heaped up. I never before saw so much white money in one place. It was a very splendid feast."

It is spring-time in the garden, the month of March, when all the flowers in their first freshness are coming up through the soft green turf by the waterside. The Emperor sits on a raised, carpet-covered chabutra, under a big chenar tree, where his presents are being spread out for his inspection: bags of the good "white money"; and those charming dalis of fruit and flowers arranged in bowls, or tastefully laid out on large brass trays, such as still grace all festival occasions in India. Across the narrow watercourse musicians play, a Kashmiri dancer swings her castanets, while beside her a sword juggler is busily engaged in going through his performance.

The whole setting is very like the garden we are considering. The Indian artist painting this picture in Akbar's reign may have actually chosen some spot in Humayun's garden at Delhi for his illustration. In any case, the tomb of the former Emperor would most probably be familiar to him; and the narrow watercourses, and little square tank with its inner circle, are similar to those still existing in the garden; where, in fact, one misses only the flowers, and fruit blossoms, and the pleasant gurgling splash of the small copper fountains.

Humayun's garden, apparently level, in reality slopes to the south, where the slight difference in the ground has been cunningly made use of to introduce tiny carved chutes down which the water ripples. At one or two places in the side walls there are longer water-chutes, where the water, which has been lifted up from great wells outside, rushes foaming down the carved stones into the garden. These marble or stone chutes were carved in various patterns, cut ingeniously at an angle so that the water running over them was thrown up and broken into ripples and splashes. Shell and wave designs were the favourites, and their name was as prettily fashioned as their carving—they were called chadars, meaning white "shawls" of water. These water-chutes are a very characteristic feature of the Mughal gardens, and were used with much effect where the ground allowed of the garden being laid out in a series of high terraces. But in small gardens, or in the plains, even the slightest slope was made use of; only a foot or two of difference sufficed to create one of these charming little waterfalls, whose inspiration was directly drawn from memories of the dancing spray and white foam of mountain rivulets in the builder's northern home.

A small pavilion stands on the terrace at the far side of the garden overlooking the plains and the river, which formerly ran much nearer to the walls. On the garden side it overlooks two large sunk plots, doubtless once laid out in parterres resembling those in the Anguri Bagh, so that on looking back, the mausoleum was seen across a blaze of flowers interspersed with cypress trees.

This enclosure, with its square plots and innumerable narrow watercourses, shows very clearly how all the details of the Mughal garden were evolved from the simple necessity of irrigation. In India the Hindus relied chiefly on their big rivers and the water collected in tanks during the heavy summer rainfall, but in Persia and Turkestan there are few rivers, so that numbers of artificial channels were made for irrigation and for the supply of water to the towns and villages. At first these Persian and Turki gardens, laid out after the old fourfold plan, were subdivided into numerous plots by the little water-runnels. In the richer gardens these tiny channels were edged with cut stone and further elaborated by the addition of small tanks and fountains. In Babar's time the outline of the garden had not gone much beyond this.

But the Turkestan Mughals were an intensely practical as well as an artistic people—as, indeed, all historical nations are who have evolved sound traditions for their guidance, and still retain the capacity for adapting them afresh to the ever changing conditions of time and place. India is a hot country, unbearably so in summer, as Babar's disheartened followers found when they tried to force him to return to Kabul only four days after the capture of Agra. But the Emperor was not to be deterred; and in their new gardens by the Jumna the Mughals in time learned to adapt themselves to their altered surroundings. For one thing, they needed more water; water to cool the burning wind, big tanks to swim in as well as long sheets of water to charm the eye with their lovely tranquil reflections. Thus we find the watercourses reduced in number and gradually widening, so much so that one can nearly always tell the approximate date of an Indian garden by the width of its principal watercourse. By the end of Akbar's reign they had grown in width until the main watercourse of the Shalimar Bagh, built by Jahangir in

Kashmir, was twenty feet wide and more. Later fountains were introduced into the canals as well as into the reservoirs, and the canals themselves became so wide that elaborate stepping-stones across them formed part of the design.

Between Humayun's tomb and the Ridge another great dome stands out conspicuously. This is the tomb of Safdar Jang, Nawab Wazir of Oudh. He died in 1754. The mausoleum is therefore just two hundred years later than that of Humayun, and almost contemporary with the beautiful Palace of Deeg. Safdar Jang's garden still keeps the ancient form : the central tomb, the four watercourses, and the four buildings to which they lead ; one of which is, as usual, a fine entrance gateway ; the others in this case are pavilions, and living rooms built into the walls. The octagonal corner towers are still to be seen ; and the garden was once full of fruit trees ; but the water-ways have changed. Instead of the small fountain basins, the great tanks, and the raised walks of brick or stone with the canal running down between them, the paths are now on the general level of the garden, while the canal itself has become four oblong tanks, one on each side of the mausoleum. These are raised above the paths and still further edged with a stone border about a foot high, so that almost half of the charm of its reflection is lost. The style, however, is still pleasing, and is well suited to the climate; but, on the other hand, it has become rather a cold, dull formality, different from the variety and adaptability of the earlier designs.

The few Mughal baghs which survive in British India are invariably those built, or chosen, as the last resting-place of some prince or noble; respect for a tomb seems to have been the only protection for its garden. Lacking this safeguard, gardens like the once glorious Shalimar Bagh at Delhi are now completely ruined.

This last famous royal pleasance—mentioned by many old travellers, but hardly even known to the present inhabitants of the city—was built in imitation of the Kashmir royal gardens and the Shalimar Bagh at Lahore, by one of Shah Jahan's wives, A'azzu-n-Nissa, known as Bibi Akbarabadi, after whom the place was named Azzabad. A contemporary historian, Muhammad Salih, gives the following account of the gardens in the Shah-Jahan-Nama: "This favourite bagh with its lofty buildings was made square three hundred by three hundred yards. The ground of its two upper terraces which is nearly nine feet above the level of the lower terrace has pleasant buildings. In the true centre of each terrace which is three hundred yards long, a canal, twenty feet broad, flows. The water of this canal runs in and round each building in the breadth of five and a half feet more or less in some places according to its dimensions, and falls in reservoirs in the shape of a cascade. The large tanks, rows of pearl-showering fountains, and domed buildings are similar to those in both the large gardens of Lahore and Kashmir; except a reservoir, in the second terrace twenty yards long and about eighteen broad with marvellously adorned halls on its four sides and pavilions on its two sides, similar to the tank of Machchi Bhawan; and except another octagonal reservoir, with a diameter of thirty-five yards and each of its sides fifteen yards with twenty-one fountains an exact imitation of the spring of Shahabad (Verinag), the water of which flowing through the third terrace, discharges into a tank two hundred and forty-five yards long and one hundred and sixty yards broad constructed outside the garden. In short, it was finished in the course of four years, at a cost of two lakhs of rupees."

From which somewhat confused account it appears that Akbarabadi Bibi must have meant her gardens to be very resplendent; combining all the various architectural beauties of the Kashmir gardens of which she, or her master-builder, had seen or heard; for the Machchi Bhawan, though perhaps it was built in imitation of the Fish Square in the fort at Agra, suggests, from its description, that the writer was referring to the garden—now in ruins—at Bawan spring in Kashmir; especially as the octagonal tank which still surrounds the holy spring at Verinag is mentioned just afterwards as having been the model for another reservoir in the Delhi Shalimar.

It was in these gardens that Aurungzeb was hurriedly crowned after he had deposed his father Shah Jahan, the formal coronation taking place later in the Delhi fort. The Shalimar gardens are about six miles north of the city along the Grand Trunk Road. Bernier mentions that the first halt was made there when, in December 1664, Aurungzeb undertook a long and cumbrous journey, with all his Court about him, to Lahore and Kashmir. It was eighteen months before they were back at Delhi—a dangerous experiment with the once popular Shah Jahan alive and a prisoner at Agra. The journey was made at the instance of the King's ambitious sister Roshanara Begam, who had been long anxious to appear, in her turn, amid the pomp of a magnificent army, as her sister Begam Sahiba had done during the reign of Shah Jahan, and also, no doubt, to see the snow mountains and the famous Kashmir gardens about which there must have been so many tales told in the seraglios of Delhi and Agra ever since the Empress Nur-Mahal set the fashion by undertaking this arduous journey almost every spring.

The Shalimar gardens are mentioned by Lieutenant Franklin, who saw them in 1793, in the reign of Shah Alam. The grounds, he says, were laid out with admirable taste: "but a great part of the most costly and valuable materials have been carried away." He also notes "the finest chanam (white plaster made of crushed marble) and the beautiful paintings of flowers of various patterns" on the walls of the harem quarters. After 1803 the gardens were for a time used by the British Resident as a summer retreat. But, unfortunately, this did not prevent their further deterioration. Bishop Heber, who was at Delhi in the winter of 1825, remarks: "The Shalimar gardens, extolled in *Lalla Rookh*, are completely gone to decay." The good bishop seems to have forgotten for the moment that the Shalimar of Moore's *Lalla Rookh* was the original Shalimar garden, not its copy at Delhi.

The garden, being a royal one, was confiscated and sold after the revolt of 1857. It consists at present of four parts, two of which still have the appearance of a garden; the others have been given over for cultivation. The depressions of the three principal tanks mentioned by Muhammad Salih and the long water-channel connecting them can still be traced. They lie outside a fine mango grove which shades the highest pool, a picturesque tank overgrown with lotus; and a half-ruined baradari, called the Shish Mahal, stands at the south-west corner of the garden.

We can follow the decline and ruin of what once was one of the finest ornaments of the capital of Hindustan. "It will hardly take a century more"—as Dr. Vogel remarks at the close of his report written in 1904—"and the little that still remains of the Shalimar Bagh of Delhi will have disappeared without leaving a trace."

One quaint survival of the days of the older Badshahi (Empire) still lingers by the Grand Trunk Road between the Shalimar and the city—the Mulbarak Bagh. This garden is the property of an Oudh Nawab, who recalled the fact that one of the Mughal Emperors gave it to his family on condition of supplying the Court with dalis of vegetables, fruit, and flowers. He cannot now fulfil the terms of his tenure; but lately he has allowed the enclosure to be partly used as a botanical garden and nursery for young plants in connection with the building of New Delhi. The Oudh nobles are always said to represent the best side of feudalism, and certainly there is something charming about this graceful action, in its suggestion of the duty of a tenant-in-chief towards his absent King-Emperor.

Nearer the city, to the west of Sabzi Mandi, the suburb of the Vegetable Market, are Roshanara Begam's gardens. This Princess ruled the Court under Aurungzeb, very much as her sister Jahanara had done in the last days of Shah Jahan's reign. They were both children of the celebrated Mumtaz Mahal; and, like her, famous for beauty and piety; but being royal princesses, they were not allowed to marry, no man being considered worthy of the hand of a daughter of the Great Mughal; or rather, as Bernier observes, the limitation grew out of the fear "that the husband might hereby be rendered powerful and induced perhaps to aspire to the crown." There were always enough aspirants and to spare when a Mughal Emperor died. In spite of this restriction, each of these ladies, in her turn, had unbounded influence, both inside the harem and throughout the Empire. Like their mother, and like their great ancestress, Nur-Jahan Begam, they were magnificent patronesses of art and letters. Jahanara's simple tomb, at the shrine of her favourite Saint Nizam-ud-din Aulia, on the other side of Delhi, shows to the full the taste and artistic feeling so manifest in all the descendants of the Persian scholar, Ghiyas Beg. The exquisite white marble grave is open to the sky; by her special request, grass alone is grown in a hollow on the top of the monument,—and where in other royal tombs the white marble gleams with garlands of inlaid gems, the "Humble Grave" of the Lady Jahanara Begam shows, as its only ornament, a lily carved of precious jade, green as the waving grass.

Roshanara, the other sister, lies buried in her own garden-house, an elaborate white pavilion with creeper-clad walls, standing on a low wide platform in the centre of the upper terrace in the gardens still called by her name. A raised canal, something after the style of the broad watercourses at Safdar Jang's mausoleum, but bordered by beds of flowers and still ornamented with a row of little fountains, leads from this building to the entrance gate.

It must have been a gay sight when the Begam Roshanara's elephant procession arrived from Delhi fort: the huge animals, with their gold-embroidered coverings, their solemn, ponderous tread, their jangling silver bells, conveying the "goddesses" of the Imperial harem enshrined from the vulgar gaze; and then the Princess herself—escaping from the noise and stifling heat of the royal palace—came in her splendid rose-curtained litter, swung between two smaller elephants, to while away a few hours in her cool, flower-scented, fountain-sprinkled gardens.

To follow in her train to-day, one must leave the dusty highway of the suburbs, with its swarming crowds and perpetual clanging of tram bells, and toil down several narrow, evil-smelling streets, until at the end of one of them the old garden entrance blocks the way.

The prospect through the dark, tiled archway is charming; on either side large shady trees shut in and concentrate the eye on the distant view of the white pavilion, with its walls and pillars half concealed in wreaths and festoons of glowing purple bougainvillæa. Every detail is reflected clearly in the placid dark-green water of the long canal; where the rose-bushes, leaning over, soften the edges of its raised stone border with their new-grown, red-brown shoots and graceful flower-decked sprays. But once inside the gateway the whole effect is spoilt by the modern carriage drives and the loss of three of the four canals. Green depressions mark the course of two of them, while a third is lost in a maze of ugly shapeless flower-beds and gravel-paths. The trellis walks and old symbolic avenues are gone—though one neglected path is still shaded by a broken pergola of vines. On two sides the garden walls are broken down; the terraced walk beside the water can hardly be distinguished; and the great tank beyond has lost its three pavilions, and almost lost its form. Everywhere winding roads driven through the old garden have cut up and completely spoilt the beauty of the original design. Even the approach has been altered to a carriage drive, through a low insignificant gate, set in a corner of the grounds; and the fine old entrance with its lovely tiles is hardly ever seen.

The gardens were obviously "improved" when, many years ago, they became Government or city property—improved after the then prevailing English landscape fashion. Putting the whole question of design—or want of it—aside for the moment, as well as that of climate, this style of gardening, good as it was sometimes for large parks and sheets of water, breaks down at the garden, even when it is a public one. All good garden-designers, whether English, Italian, Indian, or Japanese, have recognised one simple truth—to enjoy a garden one must walk. This was a fact the European landscape gardeners never seemed to grasp. The broad masses of a large English park, the stretches of autumn woodland, the banks of gay flowering shrubs, the cowslip meadows, the soft mist of bluebells under the trees, give pleasure even in a rapid passing glance as we drive or ride or motor by. But who would wish to motor through a garden?

A garden is for leisurely delights, delicate scents, delightful harmonies of colour, open spaces for games, and maybe clear reservoirs to swim in; but in India, where the chosen and recurrent theme of every art is the beauty of contemplation, the garden should indeed above all be a place of cool restfulness, a real Arama, for tired eyes and minds. It is the new roads more than anything else which have ruined gardens like the old pleasance of the Princess Roshanara, or the Queen's Gardens in Delhi City; the winding drives which give a sense of restlessness and exposure, as they cut up the garden with their broad bare gravel sweeps, and make the flower borders, however large, look mean and unrelated to each other. The beautiful canals of Indian gardens, on the other hand—the cosmic cross on which the old designs are based—have just the opposite effect. The long lines of the great water-ways and paths, hedged in by trees, produce a wonderful sense of stately dignity and peace, while the tranquil breadth of water repeats the flowers, trees, and buildings with a double magic charm, till the whole garden seems full of that mysterious beauty, that comes of the sense of calm continuance, " That one day should be like another, one life the echo of another life," which is the result of quietude, part of that rhythm of harmonious change through birth to death and death to birth again, that special Eastern consciousness of universal life.

One more old garden outside Delhi—a garden, even in its ruins, full of romantic charm—shows by its skilful choice of site, its plan so closely in harmony with the genius of the place, that Babar's great secret of success in garden-craft had not been forgotten when Talkatora Bagh was built. It lies on the lower slopes of the Ridge to the south of modern Delhi. Its walls and corner towers and three big gateways give it from outside an air of being still under cultivation, but within, it is only just possible to discover, through the scrub and thorn bushes that overrun the whole enclosure, the low terraces into which the garden was divided. The cosmic cross of the watercourses can be faintly traced with the ruins of a large baradari standing in the centre. The hummum (baths) are built after the usual fashion, into one of the side walls, and directly opposite these buildings a large tank once occupied the middle of the terrace square. So far, apart from its division into shallow terraces, it is just the usual Indian garden of the plains, delightful, appropriate, but much resembling many others. Then, through the trees at the far end of the garden, is perceived one of those elements of surprise and contrast which lend so magical a charm to these formal Mughal baghs. The upper garden wall is replaced by a long masonry terrace twenty or more feet above the lower enclosure. Immediately beneath the wall runs a wide walk, which is slightly raised above the general level, and ends on either hand in great ramps of paved brick-work leading up to the topmost terrace. This proves to be a platform about forty feet wide with octagonal towers at each end, and in the centre the remains of several buildings and living rooms; the whole terrace forming a roof-garden, like some elaborate zenana quarters in a great city palace, including pavilions to sleep in, flower-beds, and fountains.

The illustration, Plate XVI., taken from a Rajputana palace built in the Mughal style, shows an evening scene, with musicians performing on a roof-garden, where the little fountain plays amid the small square flower-beds.

The pictured garden is shut in by dark trees, their leaves patterned against the moonlit sky; but the ladies' terrace at Talkatora has the stirring freedom of a vast outlook—all the plains of Delhi melting away into the blue haze of a far-off mountain range. Pale against the horizon shine the domes, minarets, and fortress towers of Shah Jahanabad; nearer, the graceful tomb of Safdar Jang is plainly seen, and beyond towards the river stands Humayun's massive dome. Then, turning to the hills behind, at the very foot of the great embankment, lay the blue jewel of a little hillside tarn, its ripples lapping the stones of the old terrace wall, and surrounded on all other sides by the red parched rocks.

The old pleasure-ground lies desolate enough now, only the shrill cry of the peacock startles one under the trees and an occasional covey of partridges whirring past from among the rocks outside. The little lake from which the garden takes its name has been drained, and in its place a vivid green patch of cultivation shows up against the stony, barren hillside. The wells, with their water-towers standing outside the gates, and the narrow channels in the top of the old garden walls, show how the water force for the fountains was lifted up and carried along the ramparts. Possibly there was also a great waterfall from the upper terrace—a rush of white foam filling the long canal; but the thorn-bushes grow so thickly there that the original plan is rather lost. However, the garden has never been altered, and as it stands to-day even its bare outline speaks to those who care to listen of the very real sense of beauty and the force of imagination that once went to the making of this garden on the Ridge.

The palace in the Delhi fortress has perhaps suffered more at our hands than that of Agra. On the other hand, what remains has recently been very carefully restored, and the ruined walls replaced, wherever possible, by borders of shrubs and flowers, skilfully planted to suggest the original outlines of courts and gardens; and though the palace is not so picturesquely situated as that of Agra, Delhi is particularly interesting owing to its having been built by Shah Jahan on one uniform plan.

Outside the west walls of the fortress, adjoining the moat, was formerly a large square, with

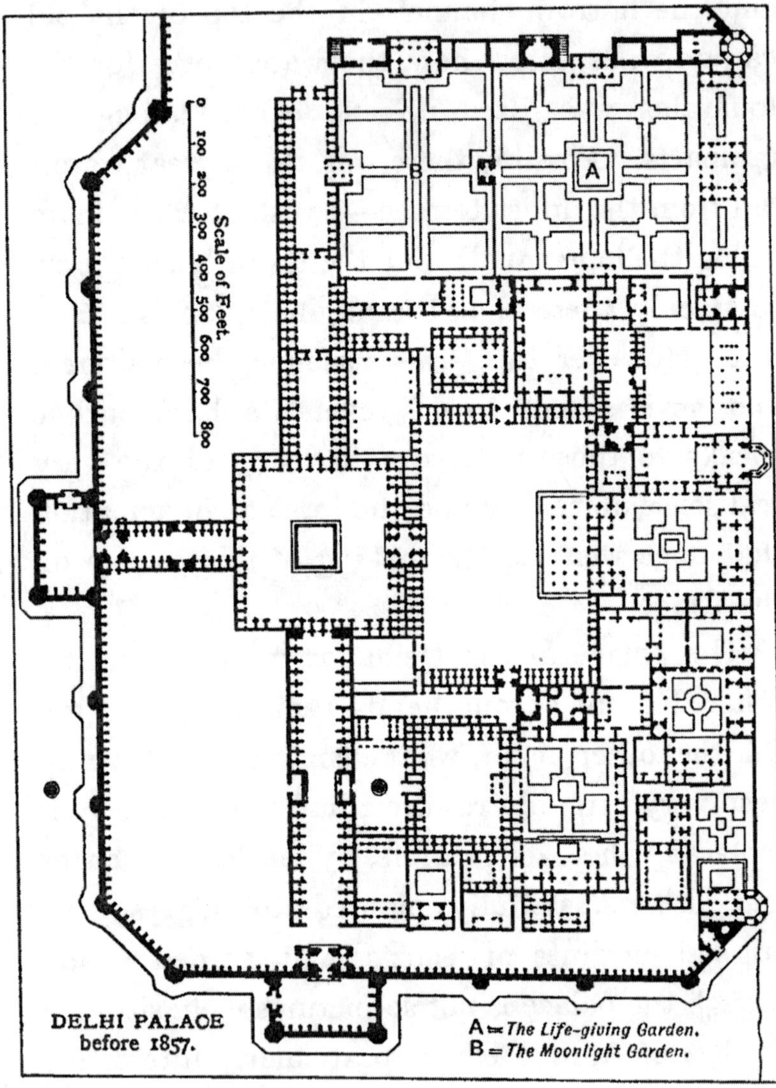

gardens on either side running down to the water. The entrance to the more private apartments is through the great court of the Diwan-i-'Am (Public Hall of Audience), behind which were originally several small garden courts, in front of various buildings. Bernier saw these zenana quarters during the King's absence from Delhi, and says that "nearly every chamber has its reservoir of running water at the door; on every side are gardens, delightful alleys, shady retreats, streams, fountains, grottoes, deep excavations that afford shelter from the sun by day, lofty divans and terraces, on which to sleep coolly at night. Within the walls of this enchanting place, in fine, no oppressive or inconvenient heat is felt."

Within the palace walls there were also two larger gardens, called respectively the Life-giving Garden, and the Mahtab Bagh or Moon Garden. Looking at an old plan of the place, before its partial destruction in 1857, showing the positions and names of these two gardens, one cannot but be struck afresh with the practical and imaginative beauty of Indian garden-craft. These gardens formed two separate enclosures treated in one design: the first was a square of about five hundred feet, the second garden-court was the same length and about three hundred and fifty feet across. The larger of the two was laid out more particularly as a water garden. The centre was occupied by a big bathing tank with a baradari surrounded by fountains in its midst. Four canals radiated from this reservoir, two of them being filled at their far ends by streams running in through two charming little marble water pavilions. These buildings still exist, and were called the Bhadon and the Sawan, from the fact that their sheets of water falling over recesses for lights suggested the showers and lightning of the rainy season. Along the terrace walk on the ramparts ran a water parterre with a fountain in each of its little beds; this finished on the north side in another larger building called the Shah Burj. Here there is a lovely fountain basin and a deeply-carved white marble water-chute.

One must have passed a long hot summer in the Indian plains to realise the full delight of this well-named garden—the joy of the life-giving dewy mornings, of the vivid transparency of the fresh opening flowers, and of the swim in the fountain-sprinkled pool; or the vast relief of the one cool hour before the daylight dies, when the grey haze steals over the fields below the river terrace, where the fountains play and the

PLATE XVI.

Tagore Collection, Calcutta.

A ROOF GARDEN.

creamy marble glows suffused with magic life. This was the Daylight Garden; while beyond, seen through its central gateway, lay the Moonlight Court—dark trees, and a white night garden full of perfumes.

The Mahtab Bagh has vanished; only half the Hyat Bakhsh Bagh remains. Looking across the garden from the river terrace a range of hideous barracks forms the background, towering over the exquisite little Bhadon and Sawan pavilions, and barrack buildings cover the Moonlight Court. The whole effect of the reception held here during the Imperial Durbar festivities was spoilt till the kindly dusk shut out the iron railings and the ugly red and yellow walls. Then as the fire-fly lamps lit up the trees and the lights of the two pavilions gleamed under the falling spray, the old palace garden seemed once more a fitting place for an Indian king to greet his people.

In other parts of the fort the garden courts have, unfortunately, lost all their original character; and the fruit trees, parterres, and cypresses have been replaced everywhere by turf and gravel paths. Still, the first view of the Diwan-i-Khas (Private Hall of Audience) seen across the vivid green is very beautiful; wonderfully so, as I saw it that December afternoon when on the platform, at one side, the King-Emperor and Queen-Empress sat in open Durbar in their mediæval robes, the great jewels of their crowns flashing in the sunshine, surrounded by their charming Court of princely Indian children; the whole brilliant group seen against the evening sky, and the apricot and amber of the gilded marble walls, where Shah Jahan wrote in Sadi's flowing Persian: "If there is a Paradise on Earth, it is Here."

This fairy palace of white marble, set on the river edge of the dark red sandstone fortress walls, was the most magnificent of all Shah Jahan's great architectural works. The Shalimar Gardens outside Lahore were another of his vast undertakings. But the real spirit of the splendour-loving Emperor seems to linger in an older, smaller building. It haunts Nur-Mahal's little Jasmine Tower at Agra, whence he looked his last on his uncompleted vision of the Taj.

The early Mughal Emperors were great builders, and nearly all the royal gardens, whose massive embankments and solid walls remain, were built in the period between Babar's conquest of India and the death of his sixth direct descendant, Aurungzeb, in 1707.

What a marvellous line of Emperors these Mughals were, six of the greatest directly descended sovereigns in the history of the world. Two, at least, were men of genius of the very first rank. Babar, soldier and artist, conqueror of Afghanistan and India, Prince of autobiographers and gardeners, and his grandson Akbar, dreamer and statesman, are the noblest and most fascinating characters in all Eastern history. For the rest of them, Humayun certainly lost ground, but he passed on the kingdom to his son, the great Akbar. Jahangir, Akbar's son, a weak man, the great Emperor's greatest disappointment, still lives in his country's song and legend in the strength of his romantic life-long love for Nur-Mahal, his Queen. Shah Jahan, a great administrator, ranks high, as must any king who inspires and builds a nation's masterpiece, and no less for that even greater scheme, the dream of the second Taj, whose realisation fate and the Emperor's bigot son frustrated. Aurungzeb was a genius of a narrower order, the Louis XI. of India; but in spite of his fanaticism he extended the Empire and held it

PLATE XVII.

THE DIWAN-I-KHAS, DELHI.

together for fifty years, by skill and will-power combined with unscrupulous cunning. Then as his iron nerve and hand relaxed in death the great Empire of the Mughals crumbled and fell, and with its downfall passed the greatest of the arts and crafts it fostered.

Babar, Humayun, Akbar, Jahangir, Shah Jahan, Aurungzeb, six famous names! But who has heard of the nine Emperors who followed? On the last alone, Bahadur Shah, in the flare of the great rebellion the light is cast, a poor old man of eighty surrounded by his mimic Court, his Empire bounded by the rose-red walls of this palace-fortress of Delhi.

CHAPTER VI

GARDENS OF THE PLAINS—LAHORE

Sweet is this Garden, through envy of it the Tulip is spotted,
The Rose of the Sun and the Moon form its beautiful lamps.

Mughal Garden Motto.

LAHORE, the northern city, seems above all others the special capital of the Emperor Jahangir and his Queen, Nur-Jahan, the Light of the World, who at one time ruled the so-called World-Conqueror, and through him the entire Empire of the Mughals.

Her name was even joined with his on the Imperial coinage, and the inscription declared that gold had acquired a new value since "Nur-Jahan" appeared on it. But Jahangir can easily be forgiven for this abrupt departure from Oriental precedent—for the coin marked the triumph of a life-long love.

Their story has been often told. To this day Indian women delight to tell it, lamenting the unkind fate which kept the lovers apart nearly half their lives. One would hesitate to repeat it, but that no account of Indian gardens or garden-craft would be complete without some further mention of the Empress who shares with Babar the credit of having designed and inspired so many lovely Mughal pleasure-grounds.

It was at Akbar's City of Victory, during one of those fêtes—a Paradise Bazaar—when the strict Court relaxed its regulations, that the young Prince Selim, as he was then called, first saw the daughter of his father's Persian minister. He was quite a boy, playing with some favourite pigeons, when he came across the little Mihr-an-Nissa (Queen of Women), sitting forlorn on the edge of a garden fountain, deserted doubtless in the excitement of the mock fair where all the prettiest of the nobles' wives and daughters were acting as traders, bargaining with the Emperor and the Begams in the most approved bazaar style. Azizam Bibi, the little girl's mother, one may be sure was chief among them all, selling for its weight in gold the attar of rose which she is said to have invented.

So the children were forgotten. And the boy, growing tired of his pigeons, gave them to the little girl to hold while he ran away after some fresh distraction. Returning presently he found one of the pigeons gone, and angrily enquired how had it escaped? "Like this," said the child, throwing the other pigeon up into the air with a scornful turn of her graceful, bangle-ladened little arms. This was a fine way to defy the spoilt Heir of India; and Selim was furious. But he very quickly changed his mind, for a playmate of such grace and spirit was not one to be lost sight of. Then as the old song tells,—"Love flitted from the listless hand of Fate," and it was not long before Prince Selim was imploring his father to let him have the rebellious little maiden as his wife.

Mihr-an-Nissa, however, was already promised by her own father to a young soldier nobleman, and Akbar would not force any man to break his word. In vain the Prince stormed and sulked; the future Nur-Jahan, even then showing signs of the beauty and intelligence for which she was afterwards so famous, was packed off without more delay with her soldier-bridegroom to an estate in Bengal given to them by the Emperor.

It seems that this youthful fancy of Jahangir's was a real case of love at first sight; and fond

PORTRAIT MINIATURE OF NUR-JAHAN BEGAM.

(By kind permission of the Fine Arts Society, Ltd.)

as he undoubtedly was of his father, he never forgave him for thus thwarting his boyish wish. Long after, when he came to the throne, one of his first actions was an attempt to recover the Lady of the Doves. But her husband, Sher Aikan, was an honest gentleman, not to be bribed by any Emperor. So a quarrel was forced on him, he was treacherously murdered, and his wife carried off to the Court. Here Jahangir was baulked again, defeated by just that very quality which appealed so irresistibly to his weak, self-indulgent nature. He had killed her husband and Nur-Jahan would have none of him. Not the least curious part of the story is the fact that Jahangir, who must have really loved her, after trying to soothe and win her by all means in his power, finally accepted the situation ; and Nur-Jahan, supporting herself by her artistic skill in painting and embroidery, remained at Court in attendance on Jahangir's Rajput mother.

Then after six long years she relented, perhaps moved with pity for the man who had lost all control over himself, and was fast losing his Empire as well. Who shall say ? Few women could resist a constancy like his. Nur-Jahan was thirty-seven when at last she consented to re-marry, after which, for more than twenty years, she virtually ruled India.

Loving beautiful scenery, flowers, and gardens as Nur-Jahan did, under her sway the Valley of Kashmir—" the Terrestrial Paradise of the Indies "—became nearly every year the summer quarters of the Court. The journey over the Himalayas was long and difficult, occupying so much time each spring and autumn that Delhi was practically deserted, and during part of Jahangir's reign the capital was transferred to Lahore, the city in the Indian plains lying nearest to the mountain barrier.

The royal palace in the citadel, like those of the other Mughal capitals, was built in a series of garden courts along the ramparts overlooking the river. In the square in front of the Shish Mahal, on one side of which stands the lovely little Nau Lakha pavilion, there are the remains of a very elaborate fountain, and several old fountain-tanks and chabutras are still to be found in the various other courts. At present the palace is partly used as a barracks; some of the buildings have been restored, but, like the royal palace of Agra, it sadly lacks its fountains and its flowers.

PLATE XIX.

SHAH-DARA.

Nur-Jahan's Garden of Delight, now called Shah-Dara, lies across the Ravi, five miles north of Lahore. The road from the city runs past the fort and Aurungzeb's huge Badshahi Masjid (Imperial Mosque)—the only great mosque in India with a garden courtyard,—and on through a dense cool woodland, out to where the picturesque bridge of boats spans the wide sandy bed of the river. On the far side scattered plantations and groups of wild palms mark the sites of many ruined pleasure-grounds between the water and the high walls of the old royal garden. It was here in the Dilkusha Bagh that Jahangir was buried, in spite of his dying request to be taken back to Verinag, the favourite Kashmir spring where he and Nur-Jahan had spent so many happy summers.

The gardens are entered, like those of the Taj, through a serai courtyard. This in itself is a very fine building, a great square with high gateways and a series of arched alcoves opening on to a wide terrace running all round the walls. These recesses formed convenient quarters for the guards and numerous servants when the Court paid a passing visit to the gardens; and at other times afforded a halting-place for wayfarers and pilgrims from the north arriving after the city gates across the river had been closed.

The tomb itself stands in the centre of the second enclosure. Its model was that of I'timad-ud-Daulah at Agra, but it is on an immense scale, and the dome was either never completed, or else has been since destroyed. The garden is a very large one, in plan much resembling that of Sikandarah. A series of raised fountain-tanks form eight large chabutras encircling the mausoleum. The canals, though still narrow, are wider than the tiny threads of water set in the broad masonry paths at Sikandarah, or those of Humayun's tomb, and are bordered by long parterres lately replanted with cypress trees and flowers.

On fête days, when the fountains are playing, the view through the great doorway of the serai—a building fifty feet high—is very fine, and will be still further enhanced when the cypress trees have grown taller. Climbing plants are well established, and wreath the walls and alcoves with graceful garlands; but the garden itself and the fine court of the serai have the usual bare look, and the avenues that bordered the wide paths and the groves of trees on the grass plots which once shaded the road-weary pilgrims have gone.

Bold repetition and breadth of treatment lend, as we have seen, a wonderful fascination, a grand, serene, and peaceful dignity to Indian garden-craft. But these vast gardens of the plains when bereft, as so many of them are, of their flowers, trees, and water, the edges of their raised stone walks and platforms left sharp and hard—casting long unbroken shadows in the blazing sunshine—easily degenerate into a tiresome, soulless formality, a tedious reiteration of bare lines. The very lines which, as Ruskin points out, when partly clothed, by their contrast form the best foil to the grace of natural curves in plant and foliage and heighten the enjoyment of the wild luxuriant vegetation—the rapid growth which shoots up after the first summer rains, the dancing sway of flowering twigs and the coloured foam of the creepers as they fall in cascades down the trees.

That monotony was the special danger of the Mughal as of other classic styles, was clearly recognised by its designers, and in great char-baghs—literally, four gardens—like Shah-Dara the four main divisions of the grounds were usually laid out in different ways. Among other forgotten charms of Indian garden-craft is the custom of consecrating separate squares, or even whole gardens, to the worship of some special flower. Such were the Lala-zar (Tulip-fields), which made such a regal blaze of colour round Samarkand in spring; Babar's Violet Garden, near Cabul; or the Gulabi Bagh (Rose Garden) at Lahore, with the motto heading this chapter on its entrance gate. Poor Rose Garden, its beds and pergolas, its very walls are gone; only its high, tiled gateway stands, reminding all who pass of the loveliness which once caused the Tulip Garden's jealousy.

Seen from the raised chabutras, these broad colour masses backed by the dark trees would be particularly effective. Poppies, lilies, and anemones were other flowers that were frequently planted in plots, and among smaller flowers, like the violets, were the red cyclamen, which still hang their dainty little heads in a row, portrayed in coloured marbles round Jahangir's tomb.

The Mughals with their Tartar traditions were great tomb-builders as well as gardeners. To explore the evidences of their zeal in this respect around Lahore is an enthralling occupation—chiefly on account of the different specimens one comes upon of Nakkashi work, that is, of the inlaid tiles so largely used in their decoration.

The whole land may be deep in dust, its details lost in the all-prevailing biscuit-coloured Punjab background. There comes a shower of rain, and unnoticed domes and ruined gateways gleam again with the marvellous hues of their few remaining tiles; a touch of sharp, vivid green among brown sunbaked bricks; the purple glaze of a little dome shaded by feathery, dust-grey tamarind trees; some lilies on a lemon ground, seen in the cool shadow of a vaulted portal; or the turquoise of a gay garden arch. The mosque of Wazir Khan, the finest example of Nakkashi work at Lahore, remains complete: an enchanting building, among whose flower-decked tiles the warning motto runs, "Remove thy heart from the gardens of the world and know that here is the true abode of peace."

Zebanissa Begam, Aurungzeb's daughter, a poetess and artist, was not behind the other royal ladies of her family in her garden building, as the Chau-Burji (Four Towers) proves. It is only a gateway covered all over with turquoise, amber, and azure tiles. Only three of its four tall minarets are left. Fields stretch behind it, a dusty high-road runs in front, but still one wonders how even a Princess could give away a garden which had such a gate. But the Begam did so, for she bestowed it on one of her friends and planned a second garden for herself at Nawan Kot, not far away. Here she was buried, and, artist to the last, by her special orders the minarets of her mausoleum were built and carved to represent four slender marble palms.

Leaving Lahore for the north, the train, crossing the Ravi, rushes by a brown dismantled building standing in the bare open fields close by the line. There lies Nur-Jahan Begam, the greatest garden lover of them all. One would rather think of her as resting by some Kashmir spring, planning out fresh rose terraces and tulip fields, or alighting at some garden gateway in the plains, like the lady in the Mughal miniature illustrated here. This may indeed be a painting of her, for Nur-Jahan was noted among other things for her horsemanship and long black hair. The turban, too, is arranged in a way similar to that shown in one of her few authentic portraits. The jewels, about which we may be sure she was particular—probably the only detail the artist was allowed to see—are identical in both pictures. So perhaps it is the Empress herself whom the two attendants welcome with the tiny bunch of sweet-scented flowers. Which of all her gardens was it, one wonders, through whose half-opened gate we catch a glimpse of the dainty white-starred flowering tree ?

Shah Jahan, Jahangir's son and successor, built the Shalimar gardens at Lahore on the model of his father's Kashmir garden. They were commenced in 1634 by his architect, 'Ali Mardan Khan. The making of one of these huge water-gardens in the plains, with their tanks and, literally, hundreds of fountains, was no easy matter ; but 'Ali Mardan Khan was also celebrated as an engineer—he is said to have been the greatest executive officer who ever served a Mughal Prince. It was he who constructed the canal which supplied Shah Jahan's Delhi, so that each house could have its fountains and its tanks ; the same canal somewhat remodelled is in use to this day. Among other posts he held was the governorship of Kashmir ; he is credited with having first introduced the chenar (Oriental Plane tree) into that country. While there he would naturally become familiar with the royal

PLATE XX.

British Museum.

A PRINCESS AT HER GARDEN GATE.

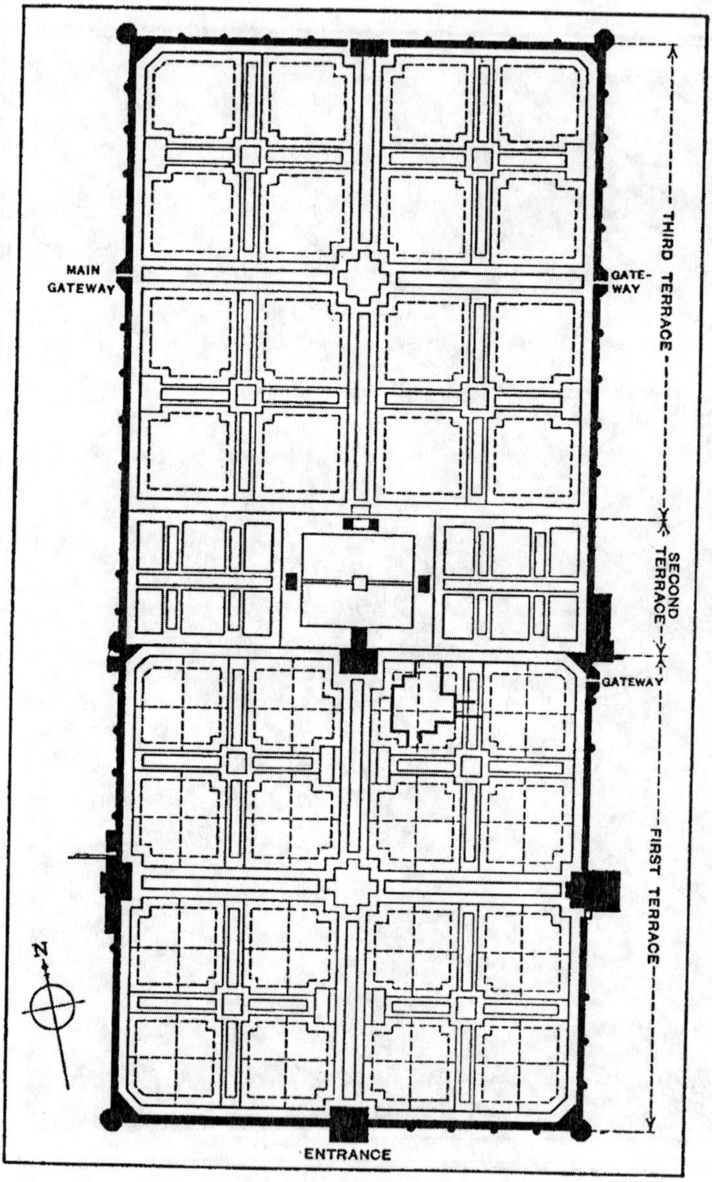

PLAN OF THE SHALIMAR BAGH (LAHORE).

garden on the Dal Lake, the first Shalimar Bagh built under Nur-Jahan's direction.

The Lahore garden, which is divided into three terraces, is five hundred and twenty yards in length and two hundred and thirty yards in breadth. Formerly, there were outer gardens extending much beyond these measurements. But as it stands to-day the garden plan may be said to consist of two char-baghs joined together by a narrower terrace, the whole centre of which is occupied by an immense raised tank. There are pavilions on three sides, and in the centre is a small chabutra reached by two stone causeways. The scale of the tank is so large that it admits of double paths and a flower parterre running all round the water.

The design of this parterre is given on the opposite page. The pattern is based on a succession of octagons and resembles the star parterres of the Taj gardens. In both cases the design was formerly filled in with flowers and the oblong beds were also planted with two small trees, such as an orange and a lemon tree, with a cypress tree in each smaller bed. This was the usual order, which was sometimes reversed by planting the cypresses in pairs between an orange tree or white-flowered banhina

STONE PARTERRE (TAJ)   BRICK PARTERRE (LAHORE)

(mountain ebony). In Kashmir and Turkestan,

a plum or apple tree replaced the orange trees and banhina.

The two other parterres illustrated here are taken from Mughal gardens at Udaipur. The Emperor Jahangir as a young man, before he came to the throne, constructed several gardens there. The first design, though probably not of his time, is in the same style which he introduced into Rajputana. The flower-beds are worked out in bricks like those at Lahore but are covered with a fine polished plaster, and the design shows at a glance the origin of the Persian floral carpet patterns. The lake water flows into the spaces forming the ground of the design. There are platforms on which to sit and enjoy the colours of the living carpet, and in the centre is a small marble pavilion for musicians. A marble platform with beds for trees surrounds the garden, and the pavilions on each of its four sides look out over the lake.

The courtyard parterre is a typical specimen of a small zenana garden. Geometric flower-beds panelled by slabs of marble surround the central tank. A perforated marble rail encloses the flower-plots, and four cypresses mark the outer corners.

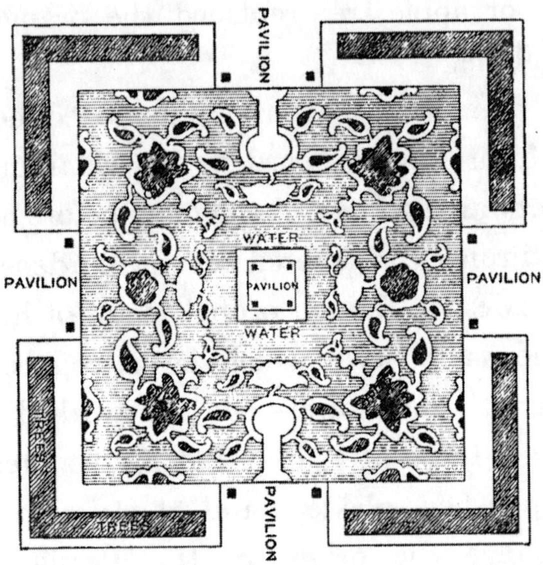

PLAN OF A GARDEN IN ONE OF THE ISLAND PALACES AT UDAIPUR.

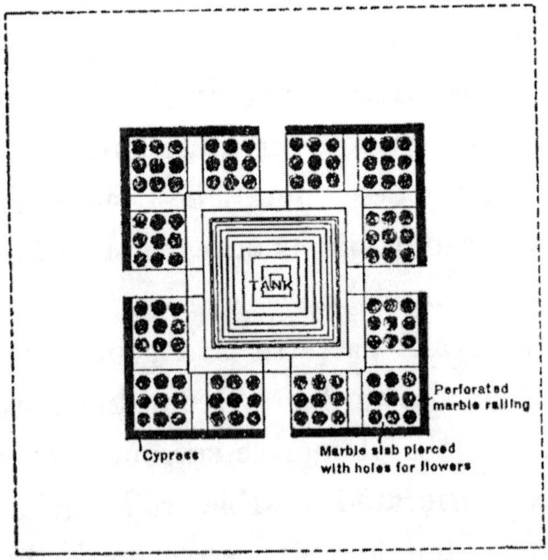

PLAN OF A COURTYARD IN THE MAHARAJA'S PALACE AT UDAIPUR.

In Mughal garden-designs the fact of the irrigation was never lost sight of, for it governs every detail in the garden. The paths are always raised, and the flower-beds sunk, even when they are continuous parterres let into the paths themselves. The garden squares are generally two or three feet lower still, and their flower-beds were planted in a correspondingly bolder way, with rose bushes, fruit trees, and tall-growing flowers and herbs. The large fountain basins and tanks were designed in the same fashion, their corners and sides being ornamented with scrolls of sculptured stone or marble. Broadly speaking, a Mughal garden is always a sunk garden, no matter how high or how numerous its terraces may be.

The canals in the upper and lower terrace of the Lahore Shalimar Bagh are wide, about twenty feet across, and they each have their line of little fountains. There are broad pathways on either hand paved with narrow bricks arranged in herring-bone and various other patterns. In the Punjab, where the land is formed from the silt of the five great river-beds, stone is not easily procurable, so brick-work and tiles are largely used to replace the stone and marble of

Delhi and Agra. These brick walks are a great feature at the Lahore Shalimar, and are particularly interesting as so many other Mughal gardens have lost all trace of the stones which paved their paths and causeways.

The pavilions overlooking the water are inferior modern restorations, in brick and plaster; the Sikhs in the eighteenth century having despoiled the gardens of most of the splendid marble and agate work to ornament the Ram Bagh at Amritsar. One water pavilion alone, called, like those in the Delhi fort, Sawan Bhadon, gives some idea of 'Ali Mardan Khan's original work. Through this pavilion the water of the large tank empties itself, filling the canals of the lower garden. Moorcroft, who visited Lahore in 1820, gives the following description of this baradari: "There are some open apartments of white marble of one story on a level with the basin, which present in front a square marble chamber, with recesses on its sides for lamps, before which water may be made to fall in sheets from a ledge surrounding the room at the top whilst streams of water spout up through holes in the floor."

At Alwar, in an old garden pavilion belonging

PLATE XXI.

THE PARADISE CARPET.

(Said to have been made for Shah Abbas.)

By kind permission of Messrs. Vincent Robinson & Co. Ltd., London.

to the Maharaja, a similar device exists for cooling the rooms—a row of small jets is placed under the cornice outside the pavilion, so that the whole building can be veiled in a fine spray of water.

A large baradari stands on the wall of the upper terrace of the Shalimar above the reservoir. The water passing through the building races down a carved marble slope. At the foot of this slope, standing out over the water, is a beautifully carved white marble chabutra or throne. These seats over the water, from their commanding position and coolness, were always the place of honour—the Emperor's thrones in the gardens. The early examples in Kashmir consist simply of one large plain slab of black marble or other stone, and serve as a bridge across the stream as well as a seat. Later, as the canals grew wider, these stones were replaced by small thrones, their legs and little rails elaborately carved, approached by stepping-stones or narrow causeways. The little throne at Lahore has somehow escaped the general destruction. The low side-rails—like most Mughal barriers, just the height on which one can comfortably lean one's elbow when sitting on the ground—are pierced and carved in a beautiful floral design. Shah Jahan no doubt sat here in state to see the fountains in his new garden play: there are a hundred and forty-four in the great tank alone. Between the throne and the cascade there is still one original white marble fountain left—a lily bud in shape, delicately carved.

In Europe, when speaking of fountains, the actual sculpture and stone-work are, as a rule, intended and understood, whereas in India the term implies the water-jet itself; although this was often a mere jet and not, as with us in colder countries, a great volume of water gushing from sculptured vases, leaping in some chosen place high up into the air for the pure joy of its decorative effect, or pouring from moss-grown shells emptied by water nymphs into pools where tritons blow their horns. In an Indian garden there is water everywhere, hundreds of little pearl-showering fountain jets cooling the burning air, their only stone-work copied from the lotus lily buds as they rise above the stream. All the older fountains in the large tanks and canals are variations of this theme. The form of the fully-opened flower seems to have suggested the shape and carving of the small tanks and chabutra

PLATE XXII.

THE OLD ENTRANCE (SHALIMAR BAGH, LAHORE).

fountains—which were differently treated, the water rising from within large shallow basins set below the level of the surrounding masonry.

On the east wall of the Shalimar Bagh, facing the central tank, are the royal bathrooms, and the four canals of the upper terrace each lead to a large pavilion; so that the gardens were fully equipped for a royal residence whenever the Emperor chose to visit Lahore. Within comparatively recent times the Sikh ruler Sher Singh held his Court in the largest of these buildings. His audience room can still be seen. It opens into a small garden square outside the main walls.

The most noticeable features on the lowest terrace are the two gateways decorated with fine enamelled tiles. The one in the west wall opens directly on to the old road from the fort, and was originally the principal entrance, for, like nearly all the Mughal baghs, the Shalimar was approached from the lowest terrace, and the topmost level, cut off by a high retaining wall with towers at the corners, was reserved for the private use of the zenana ladies.

This was a custom which added greatly to the charm of these terraced water gardens, for while the full effect of the white splashing cascades, rising one above the other, was seen on entering the enclosure, the various terraces were only discovered as it were one by one as each level was successively reached. The present approach, which leads directly through the rooms of the Sultana's pavilion on the upper terrace, certainly detracts from the general effect and character of the gardens.

To-day the whole enclosure may be described as one large mango grove; and it is difficult to say how much of the original Mughal design is left. The *Badshah-Namah,* a history of the Emperors compiled during Shah Jahan's reign, mentions these gardens. The upper terrace is described as a continuous flower-bed with plane trees and aspens planted at regular intervals at the sides. Under each tree a platform or grass chabutra was built where the Emperor and the ladies of his zenana could recline at ease. An account is given of Shah Jahan himself planting an aspen between two plane trees on the banks of the Shah Nahr or principal canal.

The description of the Shalimar given in the *Badshah-Namah* is long but not very lucid. A better idea of the planting of this and similar gardens can, I think, be gathered from a contemporary work of art, a most remarkable garden carpet which has come to light within recent years. From the workmanship and colouring it is judged to be an Armenian production of the first half of the seventeenth century. The Paradise garden of its design suggests that in all probability it was made in the first instance for the Sefari Palace at Ispahan built by Shah Abbas, Shah Jahan's Persian rival.

The design is of extreme antiquity. Chosroes I., the Sassanian King of Persia (A.D. 531–579), had a famous carpet called "Chosroes' Spring," *i.e.* garden, which was employed to decorate a hall or, more likely, on account of its great size, an open platform, for the carpet is said to have been four hundred and fifty feet long by ninety feet wide. The Arabs conquered Ctesiphon in the year 637. Nothing astonished them more, so their chroniclers relate, than this wonderful carpet. The plan was that of a royal pleasure-ground, or Paradise, representing beds of spring flowers. There was a broad flower-bed border all around. The ground was worked in gold thread, the leaves and flowers in silk, and crystals and precious stones were employed to represent the fruit and the water.

The design of this marvellous carpet, devised as far back as the times of the Assyrian Kingdom, prevailed down to the days of Shah Abbas and Shah Jahan. Since then these royal "Firdus" carpets have nearly all disappeared; only five are now known to exist, and of these only the one illustrated is in any sense perfect. But the Shalimar Bagh at Lahore remains a concrete example of the Paradise garden from which their design was drawn.

Shah Abbas's carpet is an oblong, thirty-one feet by twelve feet three inches. The characteristic canals, the special feature of the type, are unequal in length, but their form is only a modification of the older cosmic cross. The central pavilion is very small, little more than a chabutra or fountain basin set in the middle of a large tank. Four birds swim on the pond, a curious mixture of swan and royal peacock; and the water is represented as of a deeper blue than that of the canals, suggesting a greater depth; or else that the reservoir was paved after the Persian fashion with bright blue tiles. The design is further subdivided by narrow watercourses and octagonal pavilions, four on each side, representing the eight pearl pavilions of the

Moslem Paradise. Looking at the plan of the Shalimar Bagh, its close resemblance to that of the carpet will be easily seen. In the real garden the terraces with cross canals are square, but the whole design forms an oblong and in each case the central ornament is a tank. Green depressions mark the smaller canals, and eight grass chabutras, four on the upper terrace and four on the lowest level, take the place of the eight pearl pavilions.

This old royal carpet illustrates more clearly than anything I have seen the customary method of planting when these gardens were first laid out. It shows the old symbolic avenues of cypress and flowering fruit trees—which same idea was carried out in Pliny's Tuscan gardens by his avenues of clipped box obelisks and apple trees planted alternately—with their mystic birds beak to beak in the old traditional fashion, and the tulip border beneath close to the stream. Four large chenar trees are planted at the angles of the pavilions, forming an outer avenue on each side of the main canal, and trees fill the squares at the corners of the central tank. Flower-beds border the smaller watercourses and the intervening squares between the trees are filled with parterres. So without much difficulty we can imagine for ourselves what Shah Jahan's great pleasance may have looked like before it was despoiled.

The Shalimar has suffered like all its fellows. These large enclosures have been so often the camping-ground of marauding armies, while subsequent neglect and change of taste have frequently swept away the few remaining characteristics within their walls. But in spite of evil times and changes something of the old enchantment lingers round the great pool set in the mango grove, the one open square of light in all this dim green garden at Lahore.

Shut in on three sides by a dense woodland, against which the small white pavilions stand out in sharp relief, the fourth side bounded by the walls of the upper terrace, the large tank lies deserted, tranquil in the quiet evening air; rich, peaceful harmonies of pale green water reflecting deep green trees, rose-red walls, and the darker rose of amaranth in the parterres. In the shadows of the old zenana terrace, the once clear rippling water-ways are muddy now and choked with plants. The hundred little fountains play fitfully: a faint grey spray scarcely seen against the background of the dark glistening mango leaves. But as the sun sinks, and the afterglow steals through the close-set tree trunks, and streams down the opening of the west canal, where the dark battlements lose their shape, blurred against the roseate, dust-laden rays, a brief dream of former splendours gilds the platforms and the pathways, the water and the wood. And melancholy, ghost-haunted as it is, still one leaves it with regret—this old garden-palace full of echoes.

CHAPTER VII

GARDENS OF THE DAL LAKE

I went down into the Garden of Nuts
To see the green plants of the Valley,
To see whether the Vine budded
And the Pomegranates were in flower.

Song of Songs.

KASHMIR, the state which outweighed the whole Indian Empire in the estimation of the Emperor Jahangir, must have been particularly dear to the Mughals; reminding them as it did of their cool northern home-country. The whole country, however, is not very large, consisting of one main valley ninety miles long by twenty-five miles broad, completely encircled by high mountains, and when the Mughal Emperors visited it, the difficulties of transport and of securing provisions, as well as the actual dangers of the road over the mountain passes, made it necessary to restrict the number of the Court as far as possible. Only nobles of the first rank were permitted to accompany the Emperor and Empress. What intrigues and heart-burnings there must have been over the question of privilege, since courtiers not in favour were condemned to stop short at the foot of the great mountains in the suffocating heat of the Bember ravine! The summer Bernier visited Kashmir, Fadai Khan, Grandmaster of the Artillery, Aurungzeb's trusted foster-brother, was left in charge, stationed as a guard below the pass, "until the great heat be over when the King will return."

There are three old routes into the country: by Bember and the Pir Panjal; the Jumna route by Verinag; and a much longer journey from the north-west through the valleys of the Kishenganga and Jhelum. This last seems to have been the natural outlet from Kashmir and the most frequented route in early times. At Hasan Abul, where the road leaves the plains, the Mughal Garden of Wáh Bagh can still be seen. It was built here on account of the springs and used as an Imperial camping-ground.

Hasan Abul, like Bawan, Achebal, Verinag, and Pinjor, is one of those naturally beautiful spots which each religion in turn claims as a holy place. Legends of Buddhist, Brahmin, Mohammedan, and Sikh gather round the numerous springs that gush out of the ground at the north-west foot of the precipitous hill of Baba Wali.

The Chinese Buddhist pilgrim, Hwen Thsang, journeyed from Taxila to visit the spring; where he mentions the tank, fringed with lotus flowers of different colours, built by the Serpent King, Elapatra—one of those vague shadowy Naga kings whose splendours haunt all Indian history, and whose legendary doings reappear with a strange persistence in old Indian gardens.

The place is said to owe its present name to Akbar, who was so struck with its beauty, that it drew from him the exclamation of Wáh Bagh! (Oh, what a garden!) and Wáh Bagh it is to this day. But it was Akbar's son Jahangir who actually built the garden-palace.

Moorcroft, who visited Wáh nearly ninety years ago, describes it at some length: "The garden covers a space about a quarter of a mile in length, and half that in breadth, enclosed by walls partly in ruins. The gateways and turrets that were constructed along the boundary-wall are also mostly in a ruinous condition. The eastern extremity is occupied by two large stone-walled tanks; the western by parterres, and they are divided by a building which served as a pleasure-house to the Emperor and his household. It was too small for a residence, consisting of a body and two wings, the former containing three long rooms, and the latter divided into small chambers. The interior of the whole is stuccoed, and in the smaller apartments the walls are decorated with flowers, foliage, vases and inscriptions, in which, notwithstanding the neglected state of the building and its antiquity, the lines of the stuccoed work are as fresh as if they had but just been completed, indicating a very superior quality in the stucco of the East over the West. The chambers in the southern front of the western wing, and others continued beyond it, constitute a suite of baths, including cold, hot, and medicated baths, and apartments for servants, for dressing, and reposing, heating-rooms and reservoirs: the floors of the whole have been paved with a yellow breccia, and each chamber is surmounted by a low dome with a central sky-light. The water, which was supplied from the reservoirs first noticed, is clear and in great abundance. It comes from several copious springs, at the base of some limestone hills in the neighbourhood and, after feeding the tanks and canals of the garden, runs off with the Dhamrai river that skirts the plain on the north and east." The present owner takes a great interest in this old Imperial pleasure-ground, and has recently built up the ruined walls and done much to restore the gardens.

Entering the Kashmir valley through the ravine of Baramulla, the rest of the journey to the capital at Srinagar was undertaken by water. Crossing the stormy Wular Lake, the largest lake in India, Sumbal on the Jhelum River proved a favourite halting-place. At a short distance below the village a canal leads off to the little Manasbal Lake. The road to Gilgit runs along its western shore, and round the steep north-eastern banks are remains of various Mughal gardens. The largest of these, the Darogha Bagh, the royal palace built for the Empress Nur-Jahan, now fancifully called Lalla Rookh's Garden, juts out into the lake with its burden of terraced walls and slender poplar trees, like some great high-decked galleon floating on the calm clear water.

The banks of the Manasbal are deserted now,

the gardens are in ruins. Only a few sportsmen, or hardy tourists, venture their boats up the narrow canal, and anchor in the shadow of the old chenars. Fashion sets away elsewhere, toward the English hill stations, with their small log huts perched high up on the mountain sides. But the Mughals, with their love of scenery and genius for garden-building, rarely chose a better site than the shores of this loveliest and loneliest of all the Kashmir lakes.

Akbar was the first Emperor to enter Kashmir. He built the fort at Srinagar called Hari Pabat (the Green Hill), and planned a large garden not far away on the shores of the Dal, that beautiful lake which lies between the city and the mountain amphitheatre to the north of Srinagar. The Nisim Bagh, Akbar's garden, stands in a fine open position well raised above the lake; and takes its name from the cool breezes that blow all day long under its trees. The walls, canals, and fountains have disappeared; and the avenues of magnificent chenars with which it is closely planted must have been added long after the garden was laid out, if 'Ali Mardan Khan was the first to introduce these trees into the country. Fully grown they resemble heavy-foliaged sycamores with serrated leaves and smooth, silvery boles and branches. They were, and are, greatly prized for their size and beauty, and more especially for their dense shade. Apart from the garden avenues, chenars are often to be seen in the villages and by the sides of the old caravan roads. They are usually planted at the four points of a square so as to shade a plot of ground all day long, and thus formed a series of halting-places between one camp and the next. In Kashmir they still remain royal trees; they are Government property, not to be cut down without a special permit from the Maharaja. Green turf covers the ruined masonry terraces of the Nisim Bagh, which rise grandly from the water; but the trees are in their prime, and the view from under their boughs across the blue expanse of the lake, crowned by the snow-streaked Mahadev, remains as enchanting as when Akbar chose this site for the first Mughal garden in Kashmir.

Between the Nisim and the Fort there is a smaller lake, at the far end of which are the remains of a picturesque garden called the Nageen Bagh. What is left shows another lake-side garden, smaller, but in character much like that of Lalla Rookh on the Manasbal. It is built on a narrow point of land, its terraces rising on three sides out of the water which forms large canals on either hand. A pavilion shaded by great chenars stands close down by the edge of the lake.

All round the sides of the Dal Lake there are broken walls and terraces, the remains of early Mughal gardens. Hazrat Bal, the village close to the Nisim Bagh, stands on the site of one of these. The large mosque, where the hair of the Prophet is preserved, and specially venerated once a year at a great mela, is built round the principal garden-house. The narrow stone water-course runs beneath it, and through the village square, in the midst of which a beautifully carved stone chabutra figures conspicuously and still forms a convenient praying platform. The old entrance can be seen in the long line of stone steps leading down to the water, but the most interesting feature at Hazrat Bal is the carved stone fountains.

In the early northern gardens, before the canals were enlarged sufficiently to admit of the line of fountain jets which afterwards became such a characteristic, these shallow fountain basins were used as much in the open garden as they were in rooms or verandahs. Sometimes they were introduced in the centre of a raised stone chabutra; or placed at intervals along the narrow watercourses like those at Hazrat Bal, the finest of which we found hidden away under the wooden platform of the mosque. This was almost lost, buried under the mud and refuse, when, thanks to the exertions of some village boys urged on by two white-bearded elders, we unearthed this really fine example of the stone-mason's art. It is a large oval basin cut in eight deep flutes radiating from the centre; each division having a fish or wild duck carved in relief, represented as about to swim away over the edge of the fountain. A crane or stork is carved at each end where the basin is cut away to meet the swirl of the water as it rushed in and out from the narrow canal. The second fountain is similar, but smaller.

Charming as they are from a purely decorative point of view, these fountains are more noticeable on account of the birds and living creatures used in their ornamentation. This points to their early origin, when under the wise, art-loving Akbar the old Hindu temple carvers and crafts-

PLATE XXIII.

THE DIWAN-I-'AM (SHALIMAR BAGH).

men were encouraged to work again in stone for their new Moslem masters: and even these two forgotten carvings show that wonderful Indian sense of rhythm which still remains a living national trait.

The famous Shalimar Bagh lies at the far end of the Dal Lake. According to a legend, Pravarsena II., the founder of the city of Srinagar, who reigned in Kashmir from A.D. 79 to 139, had built a villa on the edge of the lake, at its north-eastern corner, calling it Shalimar, which in Sanskrit is said to mean "The Abode or Hall of Love." The king often visited a saint, named Sukarma Swami, living near Harwan, and rested in this villa on his way. In course of time the royal garden vanished, but the village that had sprung up in its neighbourhood was called Shalimar after it. The Emperor Jahangir laid out a garden on this same old site in the year 1619.

A canal, about a mile in length and twelve yards broad, runs through the marshy swamps, the willow groves, and the rice-fields that fringe the lower end of the lake, connecting the garden with the deep open water. On each side there are broad green paths overshadowed by large chenars;

and at the entrance to the canal blocks of masonry indicate the site of an old gateway. There are fragments also of the stone embankment which formerly lined the watercourse.

The Shalimar was a royal garden, and as it is fortunately kept up by His Highness the Maharaja of Kashmir, it still shows the charming old plan of a Mughal Imperial summer residence. The present enclosure is five hundred and ninety yards long by about two hundred and sixty-seven yards broad, divided, as was usual in royal pleasure-grounds, into three separate parts: the outer garden, the central or Emperor's garden, and last and most beautiful of the three, the garden for the special use of the Empress and her ladies.

The outer or public garden, starting with the grand canal leading from the lake, terminates at the first large pavilion, the Diwan-i-'Am. The small black marble throne still stands over the waterfall in the centre of the canal which flows through the building into the tank below. From time to time this garden was thrown open to the people so that they might see the Emperor enthroned in his Hall of Public Audience.

The second garden is slightly broader, consisting of two shallow terraces with the Diwan-i-Khas (the Hall of Private Audience) in the centre. The buildings have been destroyed, but their carved stone bases are left, as well as a fine platform surrounded by fountains. On the north-west boundary of this enclosure are the royal bathrooms.

At the next wall, the little guard-rooms that flank the entrance to the ladies' garden have been rebuilt in Kashmir style on older stone bases. Here the whole effect culminates with the beautiful black marble pavilion built by Shah Jahan, which still stands in the midst of its fountain spray; the green glitter of the water shining in the smooth, polished marble, the deep rich tone of which is repeated in the old cypress trees. Round this baradari the whole colour and perfume of the garden is concentrated, with the snows of Mahadev for a background. How well the Mughals understood the principle that the garden, like every other work of art, should have a climax.

This unique pavilion is surrounded on every side by a series of cascades, and at night when the lamps are lighted in the little arched recesses behind the shining waterfalls, it is even more

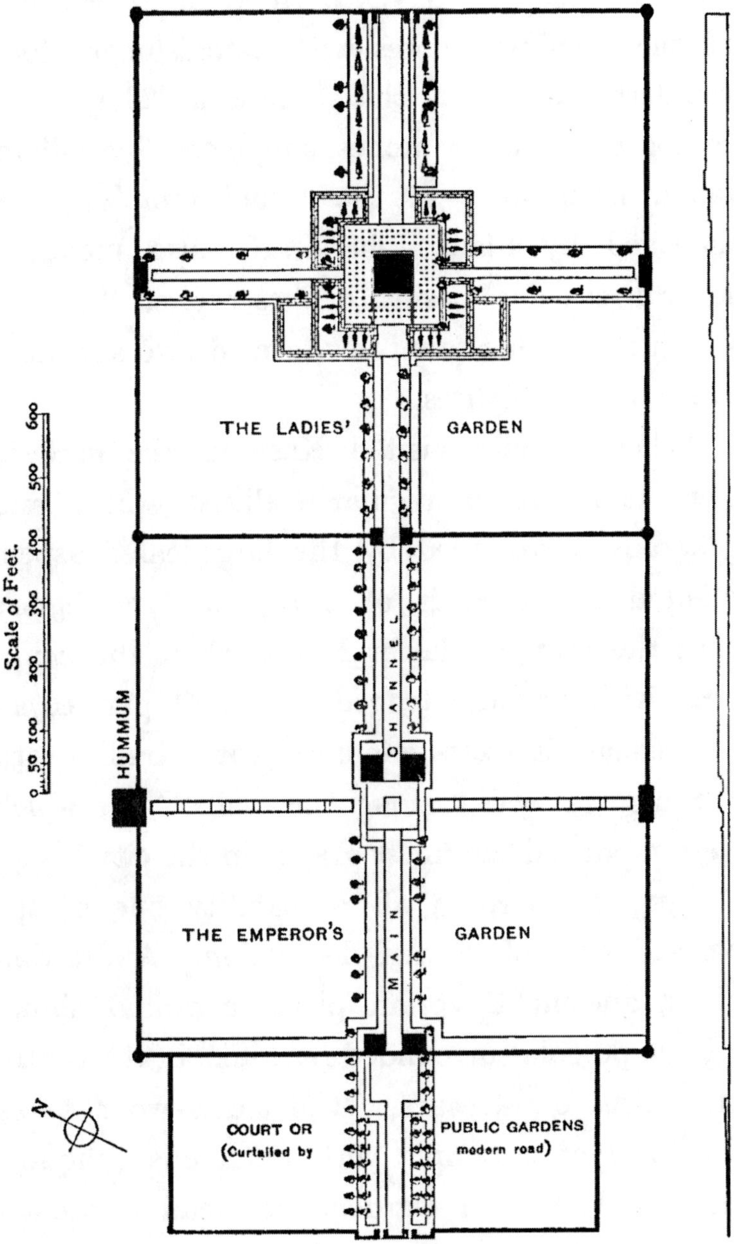

SHALIMAR BAGH (KASHMIR).

fairy-like than by day. Bernier, in his account of the Shalimar, notes with astonishment four wonderful doors in this baradari. They were composed of large stones supported by pillars, taken from some of the "Idol temples" demolished by Shah Jahan. He also mentions several circular basins or reservoirs, "out of which arise other fountains formed into a variety of shapes and figures."

When Bernier visited Kashmir the gardens were laid out in regular trellised walks and generally surrounded by the large-leafed aspen, planted at intervals of two feet. In Vigne's time the Bagh-i-Dilawar Khan, where the European visitors were lodged, was still planted in the usual Eastern manner, with trellis-work shading the walks along the walls, "on which were produced the finest grapes in the city."

Pergolas were in all probability one of the oldest forms of garden decoration. A drawing of an ancient Egyptian pleasure-ground shows a large pergola surrounded by tanks in the centre of a square enclosure. The trellis-work takes the form of a temple with numerous columns. In the Roshanara Gardens at Delhi a broken pergola of square stone pillars still exists, and a more modern attempt has been made to build one outside the walls at Pinjor.

These cool shady alleys have, under European influence, entirely disappeared from the Kashmir gardens; though here and there round the outer walls some of the old vines are left, coiled on the ground like huge brown water-snakes, or climbing the fast growing young poplars. But their restoration would be a simple matter. The pergolas with their brick and plaster pillars are a charming characteristic well worth reviving. It should be always remembered, however, to make them bold enough: high and wide with beds for spring bulbs on each side between the pillars —spring bulbs, such as Babar's favourite tulip and narcissus, to flower gaily before the leaves of rose and vine completely shade the walks.

A subtle air of leisure and repose, a romantic indefinable spell, pervades the royal Shalimar: this leafy garden of dim vistas, shallow terraces, smooth sheets of falling water, and wide canals, with calm reflections broken only by the stepping-stones across the stream.

A complete contrast is offered by the Nishat, the equally beautiful garden on the Dal Lake built by Asaf Khan, Nur-Mahal's brother.

The Nishat Bagh, true to its name, is the gayest of all Mughal gardens. Its twelve terraces, one for each sign of the zodiac, rise dramatically higher and higher up the mountain side from the eastern shore of the lake. The stream tears foaming down the carved cascades, fountains play in every tank and watercourse, filling the garden with their joyous life and movement. The flower-beds on these sunny terraces blaze with colour—roses, lilies, geraniums, asters, gorgeous tall-growing zinnias, and feathery cosmos, pink and white. Beautiful at all times, when autumn lights up the poplars in clear gold and the big chenars burn red against the dark blue rocky background, there are few more brilliant, more breathlessly entrancing sights than this first view of Asaf Khan's Garden of Gladness.

When Shah Jahan was in Kashmir in 1633, he visited this garden. Its high terraces, and wonderful views of lake and mountain, so delighted him that he at once decided that the Nishat Bagh was altogether too splendid a garden for a subject, even though that subject might happen to be his own prime-minister and father-in-law. He told Asaf Khan on three occasions how much

THE OLD ENTRANCE (SHALIMAR BAGH, LAHORE).

he admired his pleasure-ground, expecting that it would be immediately offered for the royal acceptance. But if Shah Jahan coveted his neighbour's vineyard, the Wazir was no less stiff-necked than Naboth; he could not bring himself to surrender his cherished pleasance to be " a garden of herbs " for his royal master, and he remained silent. Then as now the same stream supplied both the Royal Garden and the Nishat Bagh, which lies on the mountain side between the Shalimar and the city of Srinagar. So Shah Jahan in his anger ordered the water-supply to be cut off from the Nishat Bagh and was avenged, for the garden he envied was shorn of all its beauty.

Nothing is more desolate than one of these great enclosures when their stone-lined tanks and water channels are dry and empty. Asaf Khan, who was staying in his summer palace at the time, could do nothing, and all his household knew of his grief and bitter disappointment. One day, lost in a melancholy reverie, he at last fell fast asleep in the shade by the empty water-course. At length a noise aroused him; rubbing his eyes he could hardly believe what he saw, for the fountains were all playing merrily once more and the long carved water-chutes were white with foam. A faithful servant, risking his life, had defied the Emperor's orders, and removed the obstruction from the stream. Asaf Khan rebuked him for his zeal and hastily had the stream closed again. But the news reached the Emperor in his gardens at Shalimar; whereupon he sent for the terrified servant, and, much to the surprise of the Court, instead of punishing him, bestowed a robe of honour upon him to mark his admiration for this act of devoted service; at the same time granting a sanad which gave the right to his master to draw water for the garden from the Shalimar stream.

The old approach was by water, and the Nishat Bagh, like other Kashmir gardens, loses greatly by the intrusion of the modern road, which cuts off the lake-side terrace from all the others. The enclosure is now five hundred and ninety-five yards long and three hundred and sixty wide. Being a private garden, and not a royal pleasure-ground, there are only two large divisions: the main garden built in a series of terraces each slightly higher than the other; and the upper zenana terrace, where the wall is eighteen feet high, and runs across the full width of the garden. The water-chute running down from the second story of the small pavilion on the ladies' terrace is constructed of paved brick arranged in the usual wave patterns, and there are traces of a similar brick pavement on each side of the canal, which at the Nishat is thirteen feet wide and eight inches deep. Each end of the high retaining wall is flanked by octagonal towers, with inner stairways leading to the upper garden.

The number of stone and marble thrones is a special feature of the Nishat Bagh. There is one placed across the head of almost every waterfall. The gardens have recently been partly restored, and an attempt has been made to replace the vases which once adorned the platforms and terrace walls of all these Mughal baghs. Those already made for the Nishat are decorative and add something of the old character, but they are too small for the scale of the gardens. The Indian mali is often laughed at for his devotion to his "gumalis" and tubs,—though they are very practical in the plains, where the white ants are likely to devour everything growing in the ground,—for his crazy patchwork bedding, and his rows of untidy

THE LOWER PAVILION (NISHAT BAGH).

little pots. It is the small scale and multiplicity of these gumalis, and flower-beds, which prevents us seeing that they are only the degenerate forms of two well-known Mughal motives—geometrical floral designs and plants in vases. Beautiful carved stone and moulded earthenware garden-vases might yet be made by Indian masons and potters if they were given scope and time. Filled with flowers, their effect on the great masonry platforms would be wonderfully fine. After all, the mali has a sound tradition in his favour.

The Nishat, like other gardens of its size, was originally planted with avenues of cypress and fruit trees. On two of the terraces green depressions mark the sites of former parterres. The garden will be even more lovely when these old details are taken into account; when roses are once more trained down the sides of the walls, and soften the edges of the steps by the water, repeating the motive of the cascades they enclose. Taking a hint from the early Mughal miniatures, where the garden is "flower-scattered" like some picture by Sandro Botticelli or from the alpine meadows on the crags, which rise 4000 feet above the Nishat Bagh, let us scatter spring flowers under the fruit trees.

White iris still light up distant corners of the garden with their frail beauty. But purple and mauve iris should be massed near the lilac bushes; narcissus and daffodils planted under apple and quince trees; and the soft turf under the snowy pear and plum trees should blaze again with crown-imperials and the scarlet Kashmir tulips. The Mughal flowers were spring flowers; but roses, carnations, jasmine, hollyhocks, delphiniums, peonies, and pinks brought in summer.

The baradari on the third terrace of the Nishat Bagh is a two-storied Kashmir structure standing on the stone foundations of an earlier building. The lower floor is fifty-nine feet long and forty-eight feet wide, enclosed on two sides by wooden-latticed windows. In the middle there is a reservoir about fourteen feet square and three feet deep, with five fountains, the one in the centre being the only old stone fountain left in the garden. On a summer day there are few more attractive rooms than the fountain hall of this Kashmir garden house. The gay colours of the carved woodwork shine through the spray in delightful contrast to the dull green running water. Through a latticed arch a glimpse is caught of the brilliant garden terraces and their waterfalls flashing white against the mountain side. Looking out over the lake which glitters below in the sunshine, the views of the valley are bounded by faint snow-capped peaks, the far country of the Pir Panjal. Climbing roses twine about the painted wooden pillars, and nod their creamy flowers through the openings of the lattice. All the long afternoon a little breeze ruffles the surface of the lake and blows in the scent of the flowers, mingling it with the drifting fountain spray; for the terrace below the pavilion is planted after the old custom with a thicket of Persian lilac.

There are three flower festivals still observed every year in Kashmir, and the first of these is the lilac viewing. The lake-side by the gardens is crowded with boats when the long trusses of feathery mauve flowers are fully out. All day the people stream up the steps into the garden; and, sitting in rows on the terrace wall above, drink in with delight the sweet colour and scent of these favourite flowers. Nearly all the older gardens show the remains of lilac thickets; they were closely planted in squares divided by narrow paths through which to walk and enjoy their perfume.

The narcissus fields and tulip fields vanished —next follows the festival of the roses. The Shalimar Bagh is most frequented on this occasion. Crowds come from the city, bringing their women-folk, their babies, and their birds. Gay family parties gather on the grass chabutras, listening to the plash of the water and the sweet little piping of the birds, or smoking their hookahs and talking endlessly in the shade. Beautiful groups they make: the women with their rose and orange robes and graceful long white veils, and the enchanting Kashmir babies, their fair faces, dark eyes, and curls peeping out from under little bright green caps, from which their large round tinsel earrings dangle. One can hardly tell whether the babies or the flowers they are brought to look at are the prettier. Pink roses grow beside the water, red flowers fill the parterre which with its paved stone walks surrounds the zenana baradari. But the loveliest roses in the garden are the Maréchal Niels, which climb the grey-green walls of the Hall of Public Audience and hang their soft yellow globes head downward in clusters from the carved cedar cornice.

It is pleasant to find what a pride and

THE LOWER PAVILION (NISHAT BAGH).

delight both Indians and Kashmiris take in the old Imperial gardens. Only the Europeanised Indians have lost touch with these simple pleasures: young Rajas, "doing" Kashmir or the gardens at Lahore, accompanied by some bored English tutor, and followed by a noisy horde of retainers, walk hurriedly up one side of the stream and down the other; but even they sometimes cast wistful glances back at the flowers and the fountains, ere they whirl off again in their motor cars. Bustling sightseers, however, are a rare occurrence here, and the famous baghs are always full of real garden lovers. All great festivals and holidays are celebrated, if possible, in a garden. Students bring their books, and work under the trees. A day in one of these great walled gardens is an event which appeals as much to purdah ladies as to the very poorest class. The great Emperors who planned them and lived in them—Babar, Akbar, Jahangir and his Nur-Jahan—are far more vivid personalities in India than Elizabeth or the Stuart sovereigns are in England. And every Indian speaks with a lingering regret of the days of the older Badshahi, "when the gardens were in their splendid prime."

Lotus time comes in July, when the great flowers and leaves rise on their slender stalks three or four feet from the surface of the lake. They may be taken as the Hindu sacred flower, much as the rose is the first flower in the eyes of the secular Moslem poets; and all the world goes out to gaze on the bright pink lotus blooms. To see these flowers in perfection one must start at dawn, before the sun has climbed the mountain crags, and row out towards the Nishat Bagh, where the lake-side gardens are lost in dim blue shadows and the surface of the water is pearly grey and mauve. Then forcing the light shikara through the sweeping freshness of the large leaves until the boat is almost lost among them, wait till the sun wakes the lotus buds of Brahma. As their rose-dyed petal tips disclose the golden heart you will know why AUM, MANI PADME HUM ("Hail, Lord Creator! the Jewel is in the Lotus") is the oldest and most sacred prayer in India.

High up in a hollow of the mountains which overlook the lotus fields of the Dal Lake is the Chasma Shahi, the little Garden of the Royal Spring. Very few of these smaller pleasure-grounds have survived, but the Chasma Shahi

Bagh shows that a Mughal garden need not necessarily be large to prove attractive.

The enclosure, small as it is, has all the charm and shows the same Mughal feeling for sensation, as its great rivals round the lake. The copious spring round which it is built bubbles up in a large stone vase in the hall of the upper pavilion. The garden in front of this building is an oblong of about an acre divided into two terraces. A stone chabutra with a shallow carved fountain basin, something after the fashion of those at Hazrat Bal, is the feature of the upper terrace. A tiny carved water-chute brings the narrow canal rippling down three feet to the second terrace, in the centre of which is a tank with a single fountain jet; the water running on through another pavilion at the end of the garden. These buildings are characteristic Afghan structures on older stone foundations. Walking through the hall to the arched openings overlooking the Dal, where the wall is bounded by a black marble rail, a relic of Mughal times, the lower garden comes as a complete surprise. The narrow water-chute slopes sharply down eighteen or more feet to a second enclosure, about half the size of the upper garden. In the centre is a reservoir with five fountain jets. Round its edges are the outlines of a continuous flower parterre, and the sides of the garden are still filled with lilac and fruit trees.

There is a famous old garden saying which may be translated :

> Morning in the Shadow of the Nishat Bagh, Evening in the Breezes of the Nisim,
> Shalimar and its Tulip Fields, these are the Places of Pleasure in Kashmir and none else.

But I would add the little Chasma Shahi, with its spring, and its marvellous view, seen across the fragrant foreground of the lilac thicket.

CHAPTER VIII

SUMMER GARDENS OF KASHMIR

But see! The rising moon of Heav'n again
Looks for us, Sweetheart, through the quivering plane;
  How oft, hereafter, rising will she look
Among those leaves—for one of us in vain.

OMAR KHAYYÁM.

LEAVING Srinagar by the Jammu route, the old way was by boat up stream to Islamabad. A whole series of ruined gardens lies scattered throughout its length. In most cases they mark the site of royal camping-grounds, built for the convenience of the Court on the journey to and from the plains; while other gardens, like the ruins at Bawan, which lie off the direct route, were centred round a holy spring.

The garden, the remains of which now form the favourite camping-ground of Bijbehara, at the bottom of the Lidar valley, is by far the most remarkable of the riverside ruins. The plan, more resembling that of a garden in the plains than any I have seen in Kashmir, can still be clearly made out by the glorious chenar avenues. The trees form the usual cross on a very extended scale, radiating from what was once a large tank surrounded by wide parterres, with a pavilion set in the midst of the water. The eastern canal supplied the garden with a force of water drawn from the Lidar River, and the avenues to the north and east disclose vistas of the snow mountains which shut in this end of the Kashmir valley. The walls are broken down, but remains of octagonal towers mark their corners. There is the usual hummum, now in ruins, and the south avenue terminates in a tank and brick pavilion. Below this building is a long river terrace—a feature repeated on the opposite side of the Jhelum, once crossed by a stone bridge; and the originality of the whole plan lies in its carrying out Shah Jahan's idea of a double garden, one on each side of a river.

This was formerly known as Dara Shukoh's garden, but is now called the Wazir Bagh. The banks are steep, and the Bijbehara reach of the river is a beautiful one. The high balconied houses of the little town, and the massive forms of the chenars overhanging the stream, stand out grandly against the piled-up mountain background; and once, when the stone-edged terraces stepped delicately down on either hand, and the water from the canals fell clear over the carved cascades to join the swift broad Jhelum, Dara's garden must have had as fine a setting as any of those built by his father Shah Jahan.

Dara Shukoh, it will be remembered, was the eldest of four brothers, and the one who inherited his father's artistic, splendour-loving temperament; but unfortunately for himself and India, he failed in the more important quality of administrative ability. Dara, generous but conceited, proud of his intellectual gifts, and intolerant of advice or contradiction, fell an easy prey to the wiles of his brother Aurungzeb. In 1659 he was finally captured and beheaded; and the large mosque at Lahore was built with the funds derived from his confiscated estates.

At the age of twenty he had been married to his cousin, the Princess Nadira, to whom he remained devotedly attached, and to whom he gave the album of Mughal miniatures which still goes by his name, and forms one of the chief treasures of the India Office library. His taste can be seen in this collection of illuminations with their rhythmic line, and perfection of balanced colour harmonies; the portraits of the Emperors, the decorative paintings of the favourite Mughal flowers, and pages of dreamy Persian poetry, each surrounded by floral borders as beautifully chosen as the pictures and poems they enclose. Much Jhelum water has flowed under the old wooden bridge at Bijbehara, with the mulberry trees and elms sprouting from its piers, since Dara first built his terraced garden there on both sides of the stream. It is a far cry from his once magnificent palace at Lahore to the dark, sober-coloured surroundings, the solemn hush, and the busy scratch of pens in the great official London library; but the cousins seem wonderfully near, they live again as one reads the simple preface: "This Album was presented to his Dearest and Nearest Friend, the Lady Nadira, Begam, by Prince Mahomed Dara Shukoh, son of the Emperor Shah Jahan—1641."

Islamabad, the second town in Kashmir, stands a few miles higher up the Jhelum from Bijbehara, just where the river narrows. It is the starting-point for the Verinag-Jummu route. At the foot of the hill, overlooking the town, there are numerous springs, and consequently remains of Mughal gardens. But only some Kashmiri pavilions, and the stone tanks which swarm with sacred carp are left.

The direct road from Islamabad to Verinag Bagh, Nur-Jahan's favourite Kashmir garden, runs for nineteen miles across the rivers and the rice-fields—and a very bad road it is. For the traffic of the country goes down the new Jhelum valley road by Baramulla and Domel, up over the Murree hill, and out to join the railway at Rawal Pindi. Now, if a river washes away a bridge or two between Islamabad and Verinag, no one hurries to replace it; and the old road is left to the pilgrims from the plains or to stray travellers, such as the little company who gathered in the gardens at the northern foot of the Banihal Pass to spend, after the old fashion, the last hot weeks of June by the ice-cold holy spring.

The previous autumn I had tried to reach the gardens and failed; but on my second visit to Kashmir the journey was accomplished, and I and some friends arrived there at last.

Camped under the chenars of the ruined garden, where the pine forest runs down a steep limestone spur to the tank in which the spring rises, it is easy to understand the romantic charm of Verinag (the secret spring, the supposed source of the Jhelum, "the snake recoiled," as the literal translation runs) and the spell which held Jahangir and Nur-Mahal in their palace by the bright blue-green pool, where the largest of the sacred carp bore the Queen's inscriptions on gold rings placed through their gills. On the cold mountain pass above, Jahangir died; leaving a last request that he might be brought back and buried by the spring. But as we have seen, his wishes were set aside;—the courtiers no doubt were frightened by the approach of winter, and the danger of the passes being closed; and the Court continued their journey southwards, carrying the dead Emperor down to Lahore.

The octagonal tank built round the spring is designed to form the centre of the palace buildings. No omrah's house at Delhi was complete without its fountain court, and the same idea is carried out on the grandest scale for the Emperor's palace at Verinag. Round the reservoir there are twenty-four arched recesses still roofed over, some containing small stairways which led to the rooms above; and the few

PLATE XXVII.

THE OCTAGONAL TANK (VERINAG BAGH).

carved stones of the cornice that are left show how fine the building must have been. The current rushes out through the large arched crypt on the north side, flowing under the chief façade of the house. The stream, flashing through the gloom, lights up the dark arches with a flickering green magic like a mermaid's cave, beyond which lies the serene upper world of the sunlit water-court.

The palace is built on a succession of small arches extending across the width of the first terrace. Only the lower story is left, the rest of the building having been destroyed by a fire a few years ago. A road and an ugly rubble wall shut out the terrace and turfed wooden bridges across the canals, and spoil the whole effect, which must have been most impressive when the palace walls formed the southern garden boundary, backed by the dark pines on the cliff behind the spring. The main canal is about twelve feet wide, and is crossed by a second watercourse running immediately under the building. The garden has been a large one, although it is somewhat difficult to make out the whole plan. At present the first terrace is alone enclosed, but a broken water-chute leads to a lower level, and a big hummum with stone-edged platforms and other buildings can be traced on the east side.

For those who feel the charm of solitude in a beautiful setting, Verinag Bagh is still an enchanting place to pass the early summer days. So at least we found it; reading, writing, and painting under the fruit trees, or ensconced in latticed summer-houses built across the stream, where straggling Persian rose-bushes scented the garden with their soft pink blooms. Early every morning the Brahmins in charge of the spring came to gather the flowers to decorate their shrine. Later in the day, a school of small boys were usually busy at work in the shade of a large chenar, or were drawn up in line for a diving lesson, learning to swim with merry splashings in the clear, fast-flowing stream.

At noon even the shady garden grows too hot; and then the alcoves round the tank prove a welcome refuge, the icy water making the temperature of the surrounding court some degrees cooler than elsewhere. From the curiously vivid green depths of the tank an emerald flash lights up a polished black marble slab let into the walls, revealing Jahangir's inscription: "The King raised this building to the skies: the angel Gabriel suggested its date—1609." The mason's tablet on the west side, erected seven years later, on the completion of the work, runs: "God be praised! What a canal and what a waterfall! Constructed by Haider, by order of the King of the World, the Paramount Lord of his Age, this canal is a type of the canal in the Paradise, this waterfall is the glory of Kashmir." Brave words these, but no doubts troubled Haider—a master-builder sure of his patron and his own skill. A Hindu shrine is set up in one of the arches where the marigolds and rosebuds wreath the drab plaster walls. Pink indigo bushes and lilac wild-flowers flourish on the earthen roofs, and grow between the grey cornice stones; behind which the giant poplars whisper restlessly in the lightest breeze; while over the close, delicate, northern harmonies the pine woods brood sombre and remote. Then with a sudden burst of sound and colour, a band of newly-arrived pilgrims flock in to make their puja at the shrine. The sacred fish are fed, roses are flung into the reservoir, the pradakshina is performed. Three times round the tank they go in their saffron, mauve, and marigold robes, and the water glitters bright with all the brilliance of the hot southern plains.

Two days the summer pilgrims rest at Verinag, below the mountain pass. Then they toil on to Achibal, over the stony Sandrin river-bed, and up the rugged hill behind Shahabad, which is covered in the early summer with creamy peonies and the lovely Kashmir rose; the wild rose resembling masses of bright pink gorse—so close the flowers, so prickly their stems. The temple of Martand, on the plateau above Islamabad, is the third place of pilgrimage; the splendid ruin through whose colonnade the ninety miles of valley can be seen. To the north, at the foot of the Martand plateau, is Bawan; and far up, near the glaciers at the head of the Lidar River, lies Amarnath Cave, with its frozen spring representing Siva the Preserver. This is the goal of the pilgrimage, the whole object of all these weary months of marching. Here the poorer pilgrims turn homewards; and they are nearly all poor, these travellers by the old Jummu way. So they rarely journey farther down the main Kashmir valley, or see Srinagar, with its water-streets, its curiously carved shops and houses, its Imperial lake-side gardens, and

THE GREAT WATERFALL (ACHIBAL BAGH).

its new well-laid roads. The same remark applies to quite another class of pilgrim, who, entering the valley at the opposite end, race up to Gulmarg; and all that many of these pilgrims see of Kashmir is the forest, the faint glistening mountains of the Indus, and the smooth, green bowl-shaped meadow at their feet, where round and round the links they go, pursuing the British god of games.

Bernier went to Achibal along the pilgrims' way. "Returning from Send-bray (Bawan) I turned a little from the high road for the sake of visiting Achiavel (Achibal), formerly a country house of the Kings of Kashemire and now of the Great Mogol. What principally constitutes the beauty of this place is a fountain, whose waters disperse themselves into a hundred canals round the house, which is by no means unseemly, and throughout the gardens. The spring gushes out of the earth with violence, as if it issued from the bottom of some well, and the water is so abundant that it ought rather to be called a river than a fountain. It is excellent water, and as cold as ice. The garden is very handsome, laid out in regular walks, and full of fruit trees—apple, pear, plum, apricot, and cherry. *Jets d'eau* in various forms and fish ponds are in great number, and there is a lofty cascade which in its fall takes the form and colour of a large sheet, thirty or forty paces in length, producing the finest effect imaginable; especially at night, when innumerable lamps, fixed in parts of the wall adapted for that purpose, are lighted under this sheet of water."

As in the case of nearly all these Kashmir gardens, the lowest terrace is destroyed by the highway, and Achibal Bagh is much smaller than it was in Mughal days. But nothing can spoil the natural loveliness of this river, gushing out of the honeycombed limestone cliff, just at the point where the mountains intrude farthest on the plains. It is an ideal site. If I were asked where the most perfect modern garden on a medium scale could be devised, I should answer without hesitation, Achibal. Nowhere else have I seen such possibilities for the combined appeal of a stately stone-bordered pleasance between ordered avenues of full-grown trees, and a natural rock and woodland upper garden with haunting, far-reaching views, where the white wild roses foam over the firs and the boulders, rivalling the "sheet of water" Bernier praised.

The garden, which had fallen into decay, was re-enclosed on a smaller scale by Gulab Singh, the grandfather of the present Maharaja of Kashmir. Opening out of the south wall there is a large harem building, with a Mughal hummum and a swimming tank for the ladies in the centre of the square.

The actual pavilion through which the spring bursts out is broken down, and all that remains is an arched recess, a ruined portal set against the side of the cliff. One would give much to see in what manner the great rush of water was first confined and utilised. On either side of the reservoir into which it falls is a stone-edged chabutra shaded by big chenars. There are several Kashmiri pavilions built on the Mughal stone foundations; delightful little structures with their cream plaster walls and rich brown cedar woodwork, their airy latticed windows and their carved flower-bell corbels. They are neither as elaborate nor so fine as the older work of the same class scattered up and down the country; but they are beautiful and useful none the less, and represent a national living art, which the builders of the Srinagar villas and the pine huts of Gulmarg might with advantage make more use of than they do. In many out-of-the-way villages the old tradition lives, and the

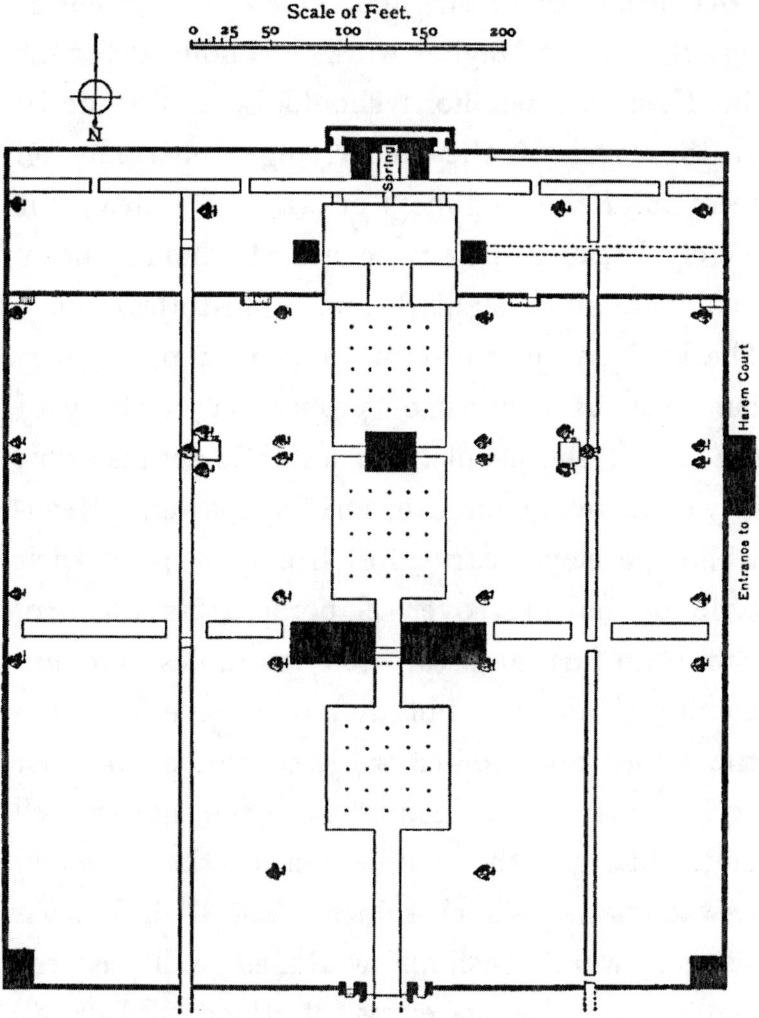

ACHIBAL BAGH (plan of the two remaining terraces).

head man's new house springs up adorned with rough but tasteful plaster-work and the cunning carving of an older day. One reads therefore, with something more than astonishment, the Report written only five years ago, which, in its archæological zeal for Mughal work, recommended that the Kashmiri pavilions should be pulled down to the level of the underlying stone, not on account of their ugliness or want of utility, but merely because they were not Mughal! Surely this is a short-sighted and unhistorical view. The antiquarian spirit in India is a pious one; but without a sense of proportion, a study of the life of the people, and æsthetic enthusiasms, it will have no force or driving power. Meanwhile the clever carvers of Srinagar spend their time on hideous, over-elaborated travesties of European furniture, tortured tea-tables, and uncomfortable chairs, not that they have forgotten the larger and bolder work so suited to their style, with its balconies and the flower-bell ends, but for the simple reason that nobody nowadays wants such things. The Delhi Durbar showed what Kashmir workmen well inspired could do. The gateway of their Maharaja's camp was perhaps not very happy—a stone temple design carried out in wood—but the high pierced and carved railing on either side of it was one of the most beautiful and satisfactory examples of modern Indian craftsmanship.

An Indian garden where each baradari in its turn is as purposeful as it is decorative, should not only be looked at, but should be lived in to realise its charms. At Achibal the summer-house set in the tank just beneath the waterfall is planned for the noontide rest, lulled by the sound of the cascade, cooled by the driving spray. As the shadows lengthen, carpets are spread on the chabutras under the huge chenars, and towards sunset the upper pavilions near the spring are used. Seen from the forest walks above the light on the submerged rice-fields turns the valley into a golden sea, on whose southern shores rise the peaks of the Pir Panjal, like giant castles, with the long, monsoon cloud pennants streaming from their towers. At night, from the gallery of the large pavilion the garden shows a vague, mysterious form; marked out by the shapes of the dark chenars, the grey glimmer where the cascade foams, and the reflections of the stars in the pools.

Old histories and stories haunt the garden: of Jahangir and his Nur-Mahal, and Majnum and Laila claim this Paradise again—he in his hopeful

PLATE XXIX.

AUTUMN AT ACHIBAL.

cypress shape, she on her rose-bush mound. For Moslem garden-craft, like Mughal painting, is full of symbolism, and rich with all the sensuous charm and dreaminess of the old Persian tales; and the story of Laila and Majnum, the faithful lovers who only saw each other twice on earth, is most frequently memorialised in the garden. Two low-growing fruit trees, such as a lemon and citron, or a lemon and orange tree, planted in the midst of a parterre of flowers, are the lovers happy in Paradise; the same idea is also illustrated by two cypresses, or the so-called male and female date palms, which are generally planted in pairs. The design of the double flower-beds in which the two symbolic trees were planted can be seen in the brick parterre at Lahore and in those of the Taj. Majnum's sad, earthly symbol is the weeping-willow (baide majnum), whose Laila, the water lily, grows just beyond his reach. Two cypress trees are frequently grown as their emblems, and the prettiest and quaintest emblem of all is Laila on her camel litter, a rose-bush on a little mound. Dark purple violets mean the gloss and perfume of her blue-black hair, saman (jasmine, which also means a foaming stream) is Laila's round white throat, "cypress-slender" is her waist, tulips and roses are her lips and cheeks, and the fringed, starred narcissus her eyes. There are other garden legends more difficult to discover, and traditional ways of memorialising well-known verses by the planting and arrangement of the trees. But the old craft is dying for want of encouragement, and we must be quick if we would secure its secrets.

Green, white, and brown are June colours at Achibal, for the garden itself has few flowers, though some of the old orchard trees have been spared; and in autumn the quince trees weave a spell of their own when the gnarled boughs droop over the water with their burden of pale yellow balls. To plant fruit trees close up to the edges of the reservoirs was a favourite custom. And a very pretty one it was. Nothing was more tiresome in the English garden of the last century than the sham gentility which spoke of "ornamental trees" as if they must be necessarily useless ones, and banished the apple, plum, and pear trees to the distant kitchen garden regions. Well, that is past now, and thanks chiefly to Japan, the orchard is again in favour. But we might have been reminded of its beauties long ere this, for every Indian garden was once full of fruit trees; Moslem and Hindu artists never tire of their symbolic contrast with the cypress; and Babar noted long ago: "One apple tree had been in excellent bearing. On some branches five or six scattered leaves still remained, and exhibited a beauty which the painter, with all his skill, might attempt in vain to portray."

CHAPTER IX

PINJOR—AN INDIAN COUNTRY-HOUSE AND ITS GARDEN

Alas that Spring should vanish with the Rose!
That Youth's sweet-scented Manuscript should close!
  The Nightingale that in the bushes sang,
Ah, whence, and whither flown again, who knows!

OMAR KHAYYÁM.

THE Mughal gardens of the plains are sad for want of flowers; the terraced gardens of the Dal have lost in part their original character; the gardens of the Kashmir springs are but shadows of their former loveliness: but Pinjor, the great garden made by Fadai Khan at the holy spring of Panchpura, still serves its purpose practically unchanged since Fadai first built this Indian country-house and its garden.

As at other famous springs, each religion in its turn has left its mark at Pinjor. There are many fragments of ancient Sanskrit inscriptions there, and Abu Rehan mentions its existence in

1030. The old name, Panchpura—the town of the five—is locally believed to be derived from the Pandavas, the five brothers, heroes of the *Mahabharata.* The legend says that these wooded hills formed the background to the closing scene of the great epic drama, and this Eastern *Iliad* rings with a strange new reality retold in this corner of the Himalayan foot-hills, where time has little meaning and the charm of leisure still survives the contact with the restless West. Here in the old Mughal palace of Pinjor, perched high above the splashing waterfalls, the sound of some far-off train alone brings back the passing of the centuries.

The *Mahabharata* tells the famous story of the contest between the sons of Dhritarashtra and of his brother Pandu for the right to rule over the northern part of India. The cousins had quarrelled, and a game of dice was to bind the losers to relinquish their share of the kingdom. The Pandavas, sons of Pandu, lost. It had been agreed, though, that if the losers passed twelve years in the forests, and another so disguised as to escape detection, they should then be free to come back and claim half the kingdom as their share. The Pandavas kept their promise; but when their banishment was over, the Kauravas, their wicked cousins, would not keep their word. A heroic war ensued. The fight raged fiercely up and down over the plains of Panipat, the battle-ground of India even in this mythic period. The five Pandava brothers won, beating the hundred sons of Dhritarashtra, and all the country from Pinjor to Delhi became part of their newly-recovered kingdom.

It takes eighteen books to tell the epic of the Pandavas, so numerous are the interwoven tales. But where the brothers hid for the twelve years before their final victory is not revealed. Local tradition, however, fills in these intervening years, and tells how the five brothers first found the spring, and took refuge there during their banishment. Then after victory, and many years of empire, they renounced their worldly conquests, and undertook a pilgrimage to the sacred Himalayas. When passing through their ancient haunts at Pinjor, four of the brothers, worn out by wars and journeyings, settled there. Only the eldest brother, Yudisthara, travelled on towards the snows of holy Himalaya and Mount Meru. He won his way through at last, but scornfully refused to enter a Paradise from which his faithful dog, who had followed him, was barred.

A gap of many years lies between this mythical history and a time so recent as the seventeenth century, when the great Mughal gardens were built at Pinjor. Their builder, the celebrated Fadai Khan, under whose direction the Imperial Mosque at Lahore was also constructed, was, it will be remembered, the foster-brother of the Emperor Aurungzeb, one of the few omrahs of the Mughal Court whom the crafty Emperor really favoured. He made Fadai the governor of this district, then as now noted for its forests full of game. Here the new governor evidently grasped the possibilities of the Pinjor spring, and, with the artistic instinct of his age, planned a great terraced garden, so situated as to embrace wide views over the lower woodlands to the plains beyond; a garden through which the spring might flow with the never-ending music of its waterfalls and fountains. Only the scorching summer of the dusty, burning plains can teach the joy and full possibilities of water. To Indians of every creed water is an almost sacred thing, and all springs are holy. Here in the Khan's own province of Pinjor was water; not the muddy yellow of the great Punjab rivers, nor the still green slime of the city tanks, but clear bubbling springs, together with sloping ground, a moderate climate, and every opportunity for a great garden. It is easy to imagine Fadai Khan's delight, and the haste with which he started planning his new country palace. But the neighbouring hill Rajas watched the work with dismay, for they dreaded the coming of the Mughal Court; and feared still more to lose the use of the precious water which irrigated the surrounding country.

A quaint story still survives, how, when at length the work was finished, and Fadai came in state to spend his first summer there, his enjoyment of the garden and its beauties was short-lived; for the Rajas quickly frightened him away. In the districts round Pinjor, and in fact all along the foot of the Himalayas, occasional cases of goitre are to be seen; so from far and wide these poor people were collected by the wily Brahmins, and produced as the ordinary inhabitants of the place. The gardeners all suffered from goitre; every coolie had this dreadful complaint; even the countrywomen carrying up the big flat baskets of fruits and flowers to the zenana terraces were equally disfigured. The ladies of the harem naturally were horrified; it was bad enough to be brought into these wild outlandish jungles, without this new and added terror. For the poor coolie women, well instructed beforehand, had told how the air and water of Pinjor caused this disease, which no one who lived there long ever escaped. A panic reigned in the zenana; its inmates implored to be removed at once from such a danger; and finally, Fadai Khan had to give way, and take his ladies to some other place less threatening to their beauty. Had it been the terrible Emperor himself instead of his foster-brother, the cunning Rajas would have met their match. But Fadai Khan, thoroughly deceived, rarely came back to visit his lovely gardens, and the Rajas and their fields were left in peace for a time.

With the eighteenth century, and the breaking up of the Mughal Empire, the Gurkas rose to power, and "came upon the hill people," as it was graphically described to me. Much more tiresome neighbours these, even than the Mughal omrahs, with their raids and plunderings over all the country round. No tricks would stop these hardy little men from taking what they wanted;

and this time the Rajas of the district turned to the growing British Government for protection. But the hill Rajas, being poor, had only forest-land to offer in exchange for the necessary guns and soldiers; while the English were then too fully occupied with troubles of their own to wish for more territory, or to look with favour on the undertaking of fresh responsibilities. At length, in 1769, after a desperate siege, the Sikhs of Patiala drove the Gurkas away, and at the final settlement Pinjor fell to their share. At the present time the little town, the great fortified garden, and the forests for many miles up into the hills, remain an outlying portion of Patiala State.

Fadai Khan's garden lies close to the main road leading from Umballa up to Simla; the long straight road, slowly rising from the plains, here turning sharply round the upper garden-wall. So once again, before the days of railways, Pinjor gardens were a gay place. Successive Viceroys made a point of resting there to enjoy the cool shade and running water, as they passed on their leisurely progress to their summer in the hills. But once more the times change, and with the change the train now rushes through to Kalka. Every one hurries on to his journey's end up in the mountains, and few know of the charming old garden they are passing, hidden in its dark mango groves, only a few miles away.

Pinjor, to others the place of the "five brothers," will always mean to me the Garden of Butterflies, as I saw it first in the closing days of a brilliant Indian October. Clouds of butterflies there were, hovering over the wild tangle of zinnias and marigolds, rising round the passer-by with a soft bewildering flutter, and filling all the sombre lower garden with their flecks of golden light; for most of them were golden brown like their favourite flowers, the marigolds. There were large brown butterflies with black veins, and golden brown ones with spotted markings; big black swallow-tails, with a sulphur band across their lower wings; and gay white butterflies streaked with black, and painted on their outer side with bars of red and yellow. One was a curious, soft dull brown, like some huge daylight moth which had been tempted out from under the deep shade of the mango trees to join its bright companions in the sunshine. Many tiny creatures fluttered by too restlessly to show their real colours; but the prettiest of all were the large pale blue butterflies, their wings veined with a delicate tracery of black.

Driving down the road from Kalka to the gardens, the highway runs through Pinjor village, where mounds and the ruins of many buildings prove that the place must once have been much larger. Many ancient tanks, with their steps worn by a thousand years of pilgrimage, are built round the springs that rise here in such numbers. One of these sacred bathing-places has been roofed in, and the remaining pillars and great stone lintels recall the seventh-century temples of Kashmir. Various old temples, much defaced and modernised, are still to be seen; also a newer Sikh shrine and a Mohammedan mosque. In this Brahmin village the last appears a sad, deserted-looking building, with its high blank wall facing towards Mecca, on which can yet be traced a graceful floral painting of more prosperous days. It is somewhat surprising to find on the opposite side of the road a large masonry tank, adorned with many ornamental fountains, in the Mughal garden style, clearly, like the mosque, a relic of the older Badshahi. Who knows who built it? Perhaps Fadai Khan, while he was making his new garden palace, in a fruitless effort to please his disagreeable neighbours.

A hundred yards below the village the road to the gardens turns off over a little bridge. It must be confessed that the approach is tame and disappointing compared with that of the great Kashmir gardens or the royal gardens of the plains. Outside the walls, an open space with a round grass plot and some meaningless small flower-beds spoils the effect—an unhappy reminder of the usual Anglo-Indian garden with its drive and "gravel sweep," so beloved of landscape-gardening days. My heart sank as I drove through it, and I prepared myself for disappointment at Pinjor. But the huge wall with its fine arched gateway was reassuring, and masses of purple bougainvillæa fell in brilliant festoons of welcome over the glittering whitewashed surface of the entrance buildings.

Through the main gateway the path leads on to a square stone platform, raised five steps above the garden and ornamented on three sides with seats built into the low brick and plaster wall. Here two fine old mango trees with spreading gnarled arms cast a dense shade even in the hot morning sunshine; and at the

PLATE XXX.

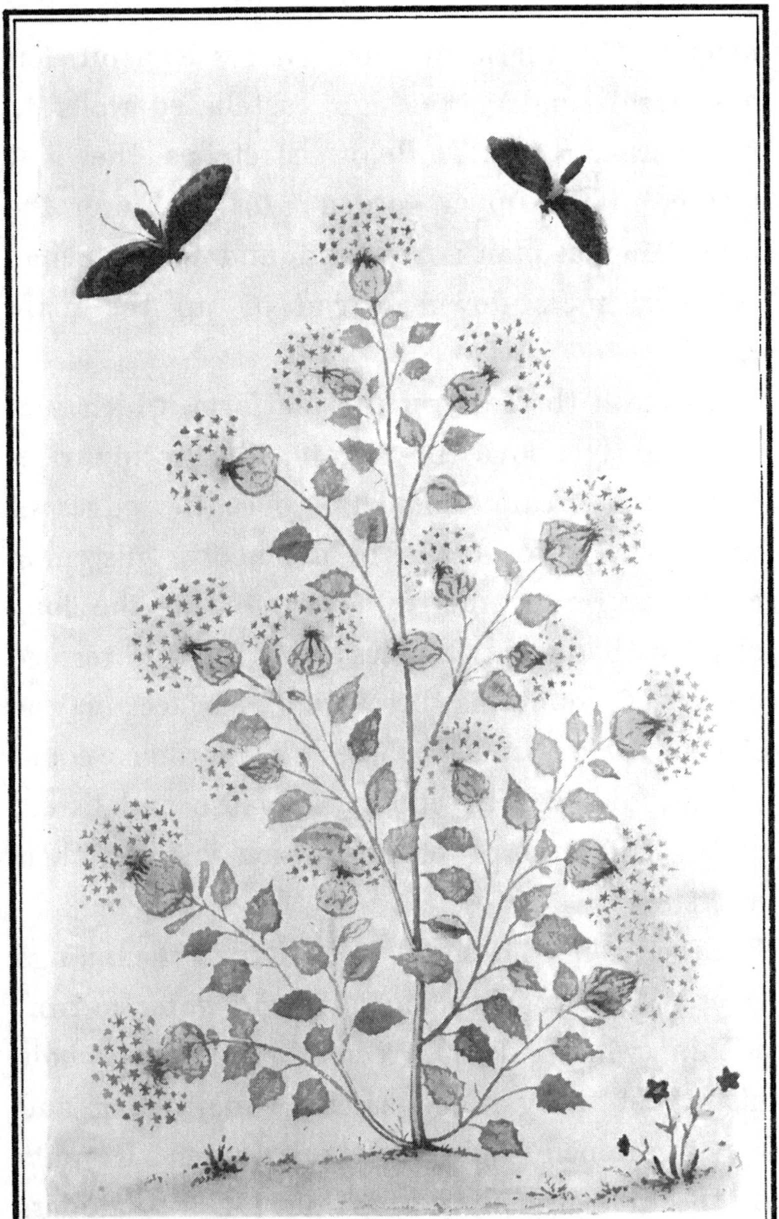

FLOWERS AND BUTTERFLIES.

(*From Dara Shukoh's Album in the India Office Library.*)

level of the platform broad walks lead off, left and right, under the high castellated walls to the corner towers. Below stretches the first terrace of the upper garden; for at Pinjor the usual Mughal plan is reversed, and the principal entrance faces down instead of up the main canal.

Beneath the seat on the platform, which juts out slightly above the stream, the spring rises through a great stone vase, over the edges of which the water pours in a smooth, glistening circle, and runs merrily away to fill the long canal with dancing ripples; and on this terrace no other fountains break the surface of the stream. How much these old gardens could tell us, did we but choose to pause and listen, of the true love of beauty which inspired their makers.

Seen from the shady seat under the mango trees, the spring becomes a magic water mirror, within whose dark green depths the whole history of the garden passes: Fadai Khan and his frightened ladies; the cunning Rajputs of the hills who drove him out; Gurka raiders rushing in in search of plunder, to find only an empty palace and deserted garden; fierce

Sikh warriors, their long hair twisted under gorgeous turbans, crowding round their Maharaja on his first inspection of his new possessions there; then English faces, white and tired, but brightening with delight at the garden's brilliant beauty. The water pictures grow fainter, their colours become blurred; but few strangers pass, and they only stragglers from the convoys marching down from the hills; native servants carrying big bundles, still, like all the poorer Indians, with a lingering interest in the beauty of old times. They stand on the little platform fascinated by the mystery of the spring. Long green wreaths shine in the depths of the water, coiling like seaweeds round and round. Suddenly, the water rising in a swirl, one darker coil flashes over the edge of the fountain and is gone. What was it? A tangle of dark green weeds floating up? The Indians would smile at such Sahib-log's ignorance, for have they not seen for themselves? It is Naga, the Elder of ALL, the Snake of the Ancient Kings, come back to claim the half-deserted garden as his own.

The spell breaks, however, as, at the garden's entrance, a hideous little lamp-post catches the eye; and the graceful old baradari built across the stream, with its curved roof and small side domes, is seen to be disfigured by an ugly verandah of corrugated iron.

Only a few big cypresses remain of the original avenues that led up to the garden-house. But close by the water, roses, jasmine, and palms still flourish, framing with their bright colours and green luxuriance, deepened in their soft reflections, a typical and charming picture.

Behind the cypress trees, stone edgings show where long parterres of flowers once made a blaze of colour, while large chabutras shaded by mango trees form the centre of the design on each side.

Flanking the white baradari, fragments of a wall remain, through which doors open on to the second terrace. This was the purdah garden for the ladies, and must have been shut out by high walls from the more public garden of the main entrance; where once for a short time Fadai Khan held his Court, and all the local business of the district was transacted. This second terrace is a hundred yards wide, and of the same length as the upper one, about one hundred and sixty yards. The water running beneath the white pavilion falls over a projecting ledge, below which the wall is decorated with many rows of small carved alcoves, used for lights.

At dusk on fête days these old Indian gardens have an added charm and fascination. Here, when the little earthen lamps are lit, they twinkle through the shining falls of water like green glow-worms; while the rosy warmth of lights within the white pavilion gives the illusion of some huge transparent shell, poised above the waterfall, its curving back showing dimly against the twilight sky and the darker blue of the mountains beyond.

Decorative lighting is a minor art that still lingers in India. At the last Imperial Durbar at Delhi one of the most pleasing features from an artistic point of view was the really fine use made of electricity for illuminations on a large scale. This was particularly noticeable in the Indian camps, some, belonging to the greater princes, glowing each night with fairy-like festoons, beautiful in colour and design; for once, a Western innovation well applied, helping to carry out a scheme of Eastern art. Beauty on this scale requires, of course, great wealth; but the little lamps might still be lighted under the waterfalls; and many other forms of Indian garden-craft revived in the country of their origin, where now they pass almost unnoticed.

The purdah garden at Pinjor and the terrace above it both illustrate the present indifference to the art of garden-design in India, and its decadence. For here, as I was informed, a "trained gardener" from Saharanpur College had been in charge for a time—the maker, I promptly guessed, of the approach outside. Inside, his handiwork was plainly to be seen. There were winding paths; the usual unmeaning little flower-beds dotted about; the same attempt at mown grass everywhere, instead of having a little laid down quite formally, and keeping that little perfect, like some square of precious emerald green carpet, such as the "grass plots all covered with clover" in which the Emperor Babar took so great a delight. There was even a tumble-down greenhouse that had been built over one of the old chabutras. Happily the gardener had departed some time ago, and the grass and trees were rapidly returning to their former wild luxuriance.

A very just remark was made to me by an Indian gentleman discussing this matter: "You

English can grow plants and flowers to perfection, and many that we never knew to exist before. But why can't you design a garden to grow them in? Look at the gardens our kings and princes made before you came."

It was true enough of modern India, but I could not let the remark pass altogether unchallenged. So I replied that, at Hampton Court, the King-Emperor himself possessed at least one fine example; and that many other lovely gardens were scattered up and down our land. But the attempt was useless—I could see he disbelieved me; for had he not been a great traveller? Never had he seen in all India such a thing as a well-designed English garden, beautiful though their flowers might be, and so to his mind such a thing simply could not exist; which settled the matter to his satisfaction, if not to mine.

We were standing while we talked under the great wide archways of the palace bounding the harem garden on its western side—for Pinjor was a country-house as well as a garden, and needed more accommodation than that afforded by the slighter baradaris in gardens near a city, to which the family or Court might go to celebrate some special festival, or to spend two or three days of relaxation. Being far away from forts and walled cities, the garden had to be built for defence as well as for pleasure, and the defences of this garden are on a very considerable scale. An outer enclosure commanding the high-road was dismantled in 1793, but the two upper gardens are still surrounded on three sides by great walls, loopholed and crenellated, with bastions at intervals, and having octagonal towers at the corners, while on the fourth side there is a retaining wall with a sheer drop of thirty or forty feet to the terrace below.

Early one morning, climbing up through what, on the garden side, appeared to be only an ornamental summer-house, I found that the stairway led out on the top of a strong octagonal burj. This tower on its southern side faced the long road to Umballa, commanding the direct route up from the plains. The masonry at its foot sloped sharply down into a moat, at the far side of which the road, abruptly turning, disappeared behind trees. The blue foot-hills quivered in the rapidly increasing morning heat. Far off, from somewhere down in the ravine, through which the road at length found its way

Lahore Museum.

AN EIGHTEENTH-CENTURY GARDEN.

to the level plains, came the murmur of the river rolling over its stony bed. Presently a tramping sound, with the rattle of jingling harness, came from the road behind me, and a brisk Cockney voice sang out, " Come on, Nur-i-Din, can't you; you chalao (hurry up) with the maachees there!"

Round the corner a little company of soldiers swung into view, coming from the direction of the village. Shuffling after them along the dusty road came an old native, his turban flying distractedly in the morning breeze, holding out as he ran the coveted box of matches purchased from the little bazaar through which they had just marched.

The impatient speaker, filling his pipe, sat on the back of a cart piled high with luggage; other Tommies walked along in twos and threes, whistling gay little snatches of song, their round, good-natured faces sunburnt and cheerful. The cool morning air and wild country round them raised their spirits; but what probably pleased them more was the fact that they were returning to their station in the plains, to their own big barracks, to their football and their hockey. Even the gaiety of band nights in the local gardens was not to be despised after a long wet summer in the hills, where maybe they had been quartered in dripping tents, at some lonely station, with little level space for games. It was a quaint surprise to see suddenly below me all those English faces, when for days I had been out of sight or reach of any European.

I think it was the big white bulldog that first noticed me. There he sat in the cart, carefully balancing himself on the top of a huge pile of miscellaneous objects, giving an air of immense dignity and importance to the whole procession. He was a nice dog, but his one pink eye and short disdainful nose were turned on me at once with evident disapproval. "What was I doing there?" he seemed to say. "Not at all the sort of place to find a white muslin frock and gay parasol. What could my occupation be?" Had he known, I fear it would hardly have improved matters. Being military, he would naturally look on art with suspicion: art—such a queer thing to interest any one; and who could wish to stay and paint in an old Mughal bagh? If it were sport, now, that kept me there, he would have understood of course; or an interest in natural history would have been easily understandable, for the study of the

Chua was his own great delight—chiefly on account of Chua's foolish habit of running round the rooms at night, squeaking with terror because (the stupid little mouse) he never had the courage to escape across the open floor. As it was, the nice white bulldog passed on disapproving.

A little farther down the road one of the soldiers caught sight of me, and calling the attention of his comrades, they halted, blank surprise overspreading their cheery faces, astonished at the sudden vision of a countrywoman of their own perched up in the corner tower of an old Indian fortified garden, away here in the jungle. But the cart rattled on, and seeming reassured that I was in no need of immediate rescue, they hurried after it. Every now and then, as they vanished into tiny specks down the long white road, one or the other would turn round, looking to see if the sunshade had disappeared. Clearly they were puzzled.

The sun grew hotter, making me realise that here even in October a morning in the garden must necessarily be short. Reluctantly, I turned to leave my burj with its lovely views and started down the narrow stairway. Where the steps turned in the darkness of the building, my attention was attracted by a cupboard door, curiously carved. As I touched it the hinge gave way, and the little door, falling back, revealed three old kettledrums. Above them in a tiny niche stood a blackened earthenware lamp and fresh offerings of flowers, marigolds and the bright purple of bougainvillæa petals. What were they doing here, and who had placed them in this apparently deserted spot? Had they been offered to some presiding deity of the garden, or to the war drums—relics of a splendid past? Or was it only the ancient Nag-worship, the Water-snake of the Spring, defying all the centuries? Like the soldiers, I too went away puzzled.

When Fadai Khan built his towering Rang Mahal (the Painted Palace) he must at least, so one would judge from its size, have meant to spend some time there, possibly all the summer months. This building is the largest in the garden, and is beautifully placed on the wall dividing the upper garden, with its two enclosures, from the larger garden below.

Like most Indian palaces, the actual closed-in space is small, for the wide, terraced roof-top

PINJOR.

was always rightly held to be the best room of the house. Below, there is a great open hall, under which runs the main stream, so that the floor space is not divided, as it is in many earlier garden houses. Large rooms close in the hall at each end, and on either side a narrow stair winds upwards to the roof terrace and the ladies' quarters. Here, on arriving, I found that rooms had been prepared for me. It was an enchanting place. Small wonder that Indian ladies feel little wish to wander in the outer world when from their purdah windows they have views like these. The rooms I used opened directly on to the platform of the main roof, the smallest of them, to my joy, still retaining the original decoration. In the lower apartments, time and a growing want of taste had quite destroyed all trace of the painting from which the palace takes its name. But this charming little room had escaped. The walls were white, plastered with the old highly-polished chanam; and the delicate designs, half painted and half moulded, brought back to mind the marble inlaid work of Agra and Delhi. The Kashmir lacquer of the ceiling shone fresh as ever in spite of the three centuries that had passed since Fadai

Khan's ladies fled in terror from their newly built palace. The little room was perfect; even the old doors were there, the woodwork painted with bouquets of flowers in vases—always a favourite Mughal design—against a dull green background. The soft west wind blew through the many windows all day long, and being nearly a hundred feet above the great lower garden, these rooms were free from mosquitoes and the deadly malaria which their bite so often brings.

Far below, all the garden seemed asleep in the warm noonday haze. On a square of carpet, carefully spread in the shade beside the water, sat the head gardener and some friends. An important person at all times, just now, on his return from the wedding of the Maharaja's last new wife, he was very much to be cultivated. There had been great doings at the capital of the State—marriage processions that took hours to pass through the narrow crowded streets, and much feeding of the poor. All night long the tom-toms had throbbed in a rising wave of sound, broken only by the roar of cannon and the up-rushing hiss and splutter of fireworks. Weeks of festivities sustained the excitement in that curious riot of noise and colour, that fantastic pandemonium of real artistic beauty and quaintest tawdriness, that form the traditional wedding splendours dear to Indian hearts. But even this engrossing subject must have palled at last, and the listeners dozed over the gardener's best silver hookah which stood in their midst.

There was hardly a coolie to be seen in the little plots of ground fringed round by the smooth, gently-waving banana leaves, where the zemindars work so busily every morning and evening. The birds were all asleep, or else the roar of the waterfalls drowned their various calls. Only the butterflies and fountains seemed alive, dancing points of gold and silver.

The sun was still high, but the deep shadows of the mango trees looked cool and mysterious, tempting further exploration. Half-way below the main pavilion a masonry platform projected into the garden, in the centre of which was a large bathing-tank. The water running under the hall above fell to the level of the tank, and thence flowed away down a carved stone slope.

From the terrace of the main pavilion the steps led down through the thickness of the fortified wall till they came out on the level of the bathing-tank, and continued in a second flight protected by a low rail of plastered brick-work. Here, for the first time in a Mughal garden, I was vaguely reminded of the vast stairways of Italian garden architecture—those superb flights of steps and balustrades that lend so much character and beauty to the gardens made by the Cardinals and Princes of the seventeenth century. Pinjor, too—the last, so far as I know, of the great Mughal gardens—was built in this same century. Perhaps even here the coming European influence was faintly felt; or it may have been only an accidental treatment, caused by the site and natural drop in the ground.

It is remarkable that so little ornamental use is made of steps in Indian gardens in general. The Mughal garden stairways are nearly all re-entrant and wind up through the thickness of the terrace walls—a wise plan obviously for hot countries; but even in the open the steps are steep and clumsy, their only ornament being the favourite leaf pattern cut on the upper edge of each rise, and in more modern work even this decoration is absent.

The lower garden was large, about two hundred and eighty yards wide by three hundred and fifty yards in length, and built on the usual plan with two great gateways in the side walls and one at the far end. The latter was smaller, and intended more to complete the design than for any use it served.

On the second terrace in the middle of the garden was a large tank in which was built a little water palace with a causeway leading up to it from the south bank, the building set slightly to one side of the centre, to leave an uninterrupted view down the main canal from the upper garden. Round the water pavilion fountains played, and on each side a water-course, now dry and filled with a tangled growth of cypress trees and roses, showed where in former days canals had led up to the gateways on either side.

The garden lay wild and neglected. Tall grasses waved down the long side-walks, all but hiding the raised chabutras at the crossing of the ways. Thickets of fruit trees filled the squares, large-leaved plantations overshadowed the walks, while here and there a stray rose-bush or cypress tree was to be seen. Alas! the old cypress avenues had gone. Still, there was no trace here of the gardener from Saharanpur and

PLATE XXXIII.

A ZENANA GARDEN.

(*In the Collection of H.H. the Gaekwar of Baroda.*)

all his works. Luckily, he seemed to have confined his attentions to the upper garden terraces, and the open patch outside the entrance gates. Perhaps the great size of the lower garden had discouraged him, and so saved the old-fashioned fruit trees and flowers. For by the borders of the long canal, here, at last, was a real Indian garden. Here were the roses and pearl-flowered jasmine, with zinnias and marigolds, scattered among them, leaning over the water's edge to kiss their own reflections. Tall palms were planted at intervals, their leaves nearly meeting across the stream, where the slender fountains shot up through them, falling back in diamond spray. In the borders the green spears of the narcissus just showed above the ground—the sweet-scented flowers which Babar loved and planted in his new gardens at Agra, together with roses "regularly and in beds corresponding to each other." His orange trees, too, of the Garden of Fidelity,—with which he was so pleased,—here they were and citron trees, their boughs bending with their load of pale yellow fruit. Below each waterfall day-lilies grew, their green leaves trailing in the little ripples. A soft mist of blue ageratum lay in wreaths under the fruit trees, and on the lowest terrace the largerestrœmia bushes had been a blaze of colour in the rains. Here it was self-revealed—the garden of the poets, of Sadi, Hafiz and old Omar. Through an enchanted door I had stepped right into the background of some old Mughal miniature. Even the peacocks and birds of its illuminated border called to me from the trees.

All sorts of friendly wild creatures filled the garden. Squirrels played among the fallen leaves. Once, when I had been very still, absorbed in my painting, a little troop of soft-furred monkeys gathered round. There they sat, like puzzled children, gazing solemnly with their bright inquisitive eyes. Suddenly, the shadow of a huge vulture slowly sailing by to his nest among the old mango trees frightened them. Off fled the monkeys, swinging lightly from branch to branch, only stopping to look down on me from safe high-up boughs. A flock of parrots, shrieking shrilly to each other, flew past—making a vivid emerald streak on the evening sky.

Twilight draws in quickly under the trees. The harsh call of the wild peacocks sounded startling and ominous. Despite its enchantment, death lurks in the garden for those who linger after sundown, when Naga, the hooded cobra, is abroad, and the air is vibrant with the hum of the mosquitoes. Unconsciously I hurried away, coming out on a level of the upper terrace with quite a feeling of relief to find the setting sun still glittering on the topmost palace domes.

High up on the tower of the Rang Mahal, crowned by the white and gold pavilion, the views were wonderful. On the east the Himalayas seemed to rise sheer up over the battlements of the old garden walls; and a thunderstorm rolling away in the higher mountains formed a lurid purple background against which the nearer hills showed sharp and clear, the white buildings of Kasauli turning to rose in the evening light. Down beneath me, the large garden lay spread out like a map, where the numberless irrigation channels shone through the gathering dusk of the trees, and the long canal with its cascades and fountains threw back the lemon colour of the light above. Round the horizon to the west, the circle of low hills rose dark against the sky-line, while to southward through the opening of the valley the far line of the plains made a distant sea. Gradually, over the lemon of the sky, a pink veil seemed to rise. The plains turned from rose to grey, a soft blue grey, rising slowly over the rosy light, and deepening into the dark purple of the sky overhead. Lights at once appeared, marking the villages on the hills behind the gardens, and higher shone the brighter lights of the small hill station. Far off a faint trail of red smoke showed where a train was rushing down to the cities in the plains. The stars came out. Lamps moved among the trees of the upper garden, all the world was hurrying homewards, and the quick magic of another Indian sunset was gone.

CHAPTER X

HOW THE LOTUS OF THE GOOD LAW WENT A-VOYAGING

A Prince without Justice is a River without Water
Or a Lake in the Rains without Lotus flowers.

HINDU SAYING.

ONE period of Indian garden building may be said to close with Fadai Khan's gardens at Pinjor. But the spacious formal garden, "the greatest contribution of the Mughals to Indian art," as Mr. Havell justly remarks in his recent book on Indian Architecture, outlived the fall of the Mughal Empire, and started on a new lease of life in the Hindu gardens of Rajputana and Central India. To understand the later development of the style there, it is necessary first to look back far beyond the times of the early Mohammedan conquests.

"Theories which bring into connexion with each other modes of thought and feeling, periods of taste, forms of art and poetry, which the narrowness of men's minds constantly tends to oppose to each other, have a great stimulus for the intellect, and are almost always worth understanding." It would be difficult to find a better expression and a sounder reason for the study of any branch of Indian art than that contained in these vital words of Walter Pater. How much of truth and value their application holds in the case of the gardens, a glance at the various influences which acted and reacted on each other there will show. Two connecting links are plainly visible: the Indian Buddhist origin of the distinctive Chinese and Japanese gardens, and the Hindu influence on the Indian Moslem pleasure-grounds.

Babar, as we have seen, was the first to introduce the Central Asian irrigated garden into India. But although the comparatively late date of 1526 marks that epoch in Indian art and garden history, the early Buddhist source of the Turki love of flowers and garden design has been most curiously brought to light by the discoveries of Sir Aurel Stein.

Gardening demands, perhaps more than any other art, peace and leisure, tranquillity and patience, and in every age and country the pioneers and early masters of the craft have been religious teachers and monks. The Hindus and Buddhists, with their wide sympathies and their simple, joyous love of nature, made much use of flowers in their religious ritual. Their monks and missioners travelled far and wide, and with them the Lotus of the Good Law went voyaging into many lands. What the mihrab, Allah as a spirit, invisible, intangible, is to the Mohammedans, the Cross of Redemption to the Christians, the Lotus is to the Buddhist and Hindu. A lotus floating on the cosmic waters is the symbol of the creation of the world. Three species of the flower grow in India : the *Nymphæa Lotus*, the white Lotus of ancient Egypt ; the *Nymphæa caerulea*, the blue species ; and the *Nelumbium speciosum*, the rose-coloured or sacred Lotus of India, which, Professor Joret believes, only entered Egypt in the times of the Ptolemies. Each colour is sacred to one aspect of the Trinity : the rose-petaled lotus—that of the Dal Lake—is the flower of sunrise, Brahma's prayer ; the blue flower is sacred to Vishnu, upholder of the blue noontide universe ; the white lotus of evening is the flower of death and

PLATE XXXIV.

BHARATPUR PALACE GARDEN.

resurrection, the emblem of Siva, the Destroyer and Preserver. On a Lotus the Good Law floated to Java, and its flowering can be seen to this day at Borobudur. It was carried south to Cambodia, and Angkor Vat is still the largest temple in the world. Northwards and eastwards the Sacred Lotus journeyed, and the wind and the covering sand followed in its wake; so that the road was well-nigh forgotten when Sir Aurel Stein found the frescoes of Vishnu's dark blue flowers, and the little garden buried in the waste. Farther and farther the flower travelled till China and Japan owned its sway, and India, the home of the lotus, the land of Buddha and of Rama, is still the Holy Land of all the Further East.

The Indian flora, so unlike that of Central Asia, together with the difference of climate, gave a very distinctive character to the Hindu and Buddhist garden. Strange as it may seem, there are few wild flowers found growing in the Indian plains; for there, even in winter, the fierce sun burns into the soil. But the flower patches of the northern hills and meadows are replaced by deep-rooted blossoming trees, and these make up to some extent for the absence of the smaller herbaceous plants. Their leafless boughs and bare twigs burst into gorgeous flowering in the hot Indian spring, till the jungle glows like English beech and elm woods on a clear autumn day. Then in the plains there is the second flowering, the season of the rains, when the rank green growth chokes all but the tall grasses and ferns, and the lotus flowers with their lovely curving leaves completely hide the surface of the ponds. Creepers flourish in the damp dripping forests, where the gnarled twisted limbs of the old mangoes are fringed with sweet scented orchid sprays, as if swarms of little mauve and yellow butterflies were fluttering down to settle in the shadows of the trees. But the orchids of the Himalayan forests and Nilghiri hills, in spite of their strange beauty of form and colour, failed to win a place in the Indian garden. Even that wonderful lily, the *Gloriosa superba,* seems to have passed unnoticed, and the rose, although a wild flower in the north-western mountains, did not find its way into Hindu parterres until after the Mohammedan conquest. Amaranth and the tulsi, "Holy Basil," are practically the only herbaceous flowers mentioned in the old Indian stories and plays.

The Hindu Arama was then a cool woodland

place, full of thick foliaged trees and shrubs gay with brilliant, perfumed flowers. The shady alleys were kept cleared and swept. Evergreens were clipped and trained to form aromatic scented bowers over platforms paved with fine mosaic. Creepers wreathed the white garden-houses, whose inner walls were covered with frescoes. The heroines of old did not disdain to plant and water their favourite trees with their own hands. Indeed it was held that the asoka—sorrow allaying—tree, whose splendid orange-red flowers are sacred to the Lord Siva, never flowered to perfection unless its roots had first been pressed by the foot of a beautiful young girl. This ceremony, a charming allegory of spring, is a frequent motive with the poets and temple carvers. These woodland gardens were full of lotus ponds, but as far as I know there is no mention of the old symbolic four-went water-ways, although the references to fountains would suggest that the water must have been running. But the artificial "Pleasure Hill," as it was called, placed in the centre of the ground, definitely connects the Hindu garden, like that of Central Asia, with the ancient symbolism of the Holy Mount, the Tree, and the Snake.

Almost everything Indian may be traced back to the Mahabharata or Ramayana—if not further still—and both these great epics show the national Hindu feeling of close harmony with nature and love for all created things. There are constant references in these poems to flowers and gardens, and a garden or forest grove forms the background in nearly every scene. As a rule these landscape pictures are somewhat vague and shadowy, but a description in the Mahabharata, translated by Professor Joret in his book, *Les Plantes dans l'antiquité et au moyen âge*, of the pleasure-grounds surrounding Kandavaprastha, the capital of the Pandavas, is more definite. The gardens were "ornamented in all seasons with flowers and fruits." Among the various trees and plants mentioned are the mango, asoka, champaka, nag-champa, sal tree, palmyra tree, skrew pine, bignonia, coral tree, and oleander. All kinds of birds frequented the gardens, which "re-echoed to the cry of the peacock and the song of the kokila"—Indian cuckoo. "The walls of the pavilions shone like mirrors. There were numerous arbours covered by creepers, charming artificial hillocks, lakes filled to the brim with clear water, fish ponds carpeted with

PLATE XXXV.

THE LILAC TERRACE (NISHAT BAGH).

lotus and water lilies, and ponds, covered by delicate aquatic plants, on which swam red geese, ducks, and swans."

The early Indian gardens were evolved very much on the lines that the climate and flowers of thc plains would lead us to expect. Apart from the Pleasure Hill, their outstanding features were the flowering trees, the creepers, and the aquatic plants; the mango, asoka, and champaka groves, the bignonia, jasmine, and convolvulus bowers, and the lotus and water lilies floating on the ponds. Along the foot of the Himalayas, in Bengal, Burmah, Cambodia, and Java, gardens such as these flourished until, as we have seen, the coming of the Mughals changed the aspect of the Indian gardens. Once introduced, the new fashion took firm hold, for the Central Asian water-garden based on the system of irrigation was one specially suited to the arid plains of Upper India and the dry red rocks of the Rajputana hills.

The Indian Buddhist garden, forgotten in the land of its origin, still survives further East, although so transformed and tinged by the genius of another climate and another people, that the garden history of the plum and cherry tree, the wisteria and morning glory, the lotus and Japanese iris, is often misunderstood and overlooked. For all that, the Japanese garden, the most intimate and charming expression of Japanese nationality, came like so many of their arts from India through China and Korea. And from the early temple gardens made by the Buddhist monks and pilgrims, the whole beautiful and elaborate system of Japanese garden craft has gradually been built up.

The Indian Lotus-bearers reached China both through Turkestan and by the southern route through Burmah and Cambodia, and "Coal Hill," near the Tatar city in Peking, is a relic of the Pleasure Hill idea. The style is supposed to have been introduced into Japan in the sixth century by one Yohan Koan Han, who constructed great mounds, some of them a hundred feet high or more, and brought water in conduits to form lakes and ponds. These hills and rockeries were planted after the Indian fashion with flowering trees and shrubs. True, before this date the Japanese had a garden style called "Imperial Hall," from a famous royal garden, a quadrangle enclosed on three sides by palace buildings, but not much is known of the details of the style except that there was an irregular lake with an island and a little bridge connecting it with the shore. But the Plum and Orange tree right and left of the entrance to the palace are strangely reminiscent of the ancient Hindu marriage of the fruit trees by the garden well. The flowers show still more strangely the persistence of the old ideas, for in a land of wonderful wild flowers half the gardens in Japan are green gardens, and, except for the blossoming trees and shrubs, the lotus in the pond, the iris fringing its margin, and the wisteria on the trellis overhead, all the garden flowers are in pots. The old traditional flowers seem the only ones to take root in the garden soil. Peonies, lilies, asters, and other more recently introduced flowers are all planted in pots. Even the national chrysanthemum, whose curving petals represent the wheel of the Buddhist Law and the rays of the rising sun, is not grown in the ground, but is invariably set out in blue and white or pale green flower pots.

It is still more interesting to trace the influence of climate on Buddhist garden building, how it expanded in the moist atmosphere of Japan where the rainfall is twice as heavy as it is even in our own rainy islands; and where the frequent danger of earthquakes and the consequent use of wooden buildings must not be lost sight of.

The Japanese landscape garden suffers with us to some extent from its name, for unlike the English landscape style, which had only a mistaken romanticism behind it, garden craft in Japan is as exquisitely balanced and restrained in its harmony of house and garden as is the most formal old English pleasance or stately Mughal bagh. Throughout every Japanese garden, from the largest to the smallest, the scale of the whole design is strictly maintained, so that the house, the garden gates, the enclosing railings, even the stone lanterns, all combine to enhance and emphasise its general character. So strong is the national feeling for beauty in its real sense of balance and unity, that the most valuable garden ornament may be worthless in the eyes of the owner of a simple garden.

Far as the Lotus travelled in Asia, its journeys were not completed there, for within recent years its spirit entered English gardens with the advent of the Japanese iris. Fresh points of view and a change of technique give an impetus to every art; details may with advantage be transplanted and transformed; but regardless of climate, to try and transplant bodily a whole national style, whether it be from Japan to England, or from England back to India, is an obvious mistake. Yet so-called Japanese gardens are planted in England without the spirit of their Buddhist symbolism, or the need of their wooden earthquake-proof houses; open mid-Victorian parks and gardens are planned in India without the possibilities of the flowers in the long grass and the fine green English turf; when all the time, climate and nationality are the very pith and soul of garden craft, just as character is the core of individual personal charm.

CHAPTER XI

MOONLIGHT GARDENS, AND THE PALACE OF DEEG

Sois content des fleurs, des fruits, même des feuilles,
Si dans ton jardin à toi tu les cueilles.

EDMOND ROSTAND.

THE Indian Buddhists were great gardeners, and evidence of their skill may yet be seen in places like the "Lanoli Grove" beyond Khandalla on the railway line between Bombay and Poona, which is full of rare trees and flowering shrubs found nowhere else in Western India. The spot was at one time a Buddhist shrine, and the foreign trees are without doubt survivals of an ancient temple enclosure or grove. Sir George Birdwood tells me of another such place at Chembur on the island of Trombay opposite Salsette, where he found near some ruins, said to be of a Buddhist site, a solitary white pangri tree (*Erythrina indica*) from which he took many cuttings, dis-

PLATE XXXVI.

THE GARDEN-PALACE OF DEEG.

tributing them among friends in different parts of India.

Of all Hindu sects the Jains are the nearest to the Buddhists of ancient India in their keen sense of the universal indwelling soul of things; and the Jains and Vaeshnavas, more than other Hindus, set store by their gardens. Nearly all the bankers and rich merchants of Western India belong to one or the other of these divisions of Hinduism. It cannot be said that they are now strict in laying out their actual gardens in accordance with their paradisiacal ideal of them, and so long as their garden is a paradise to their soul and their spiritual eye, they are not so particular as were the Mughals about its being truly "four square."

In the same way, when the Hindu princes and wealthy merchants build their great mansions and palaces with their numerous arched openings, they delight to call them "the chaurasi," a name derived from the number eighty-four, a multiple of twelve (the number of the signs of the zodiac) by seven (the number of the planets); but the particular palace may have only fifty or sixty openings in reality. This number, eighty-four, is a most sacred one with Hindus and

Buddhists alike, so much so that, to quote Sir George Birdwood again: "If a man live to eighty-four he is by that fact alone constituted a saint, however big a blackguard he may have been—or still prefer to be."

According to an old Indian treatise on gardening, five trees should be first planted, as they are luck bringing—phalsa (*Grewia asiatica*), bhila or marking-nut tree, punag (*Rottlera tinctoria*), sirisha (*Mimosa Sirissa*), and nim (*Melia Azardirachta*); after this, plantations of any kind can be made. The auspicious sides for planting are: on the east the bur (*Ficus indica*) and karanda (*Carissa Carandas*); on the south gular (*Ficus glomerata*) and bambu; on the west amalaka (*Emblica officinalis*) and bila (*Aegle Marmelos*); on the north pakar (*Ficus infectoria*), bhor (*Zizyphus Jujuba*), and kaitha (*Feronica Elephantum*). The bur tree should not be planted at the gate of the house or in such a place that the shadow of it may fall on the building. All large trees are inauspicious within the house, *i.e.* in the central courtyard, particularly those of a thorny nature—a sensible rule, as is that which prescribes the cool north side of the mansion as the most propitious on which to lay out the garden. If the "nim-tree"—one of the "lucky" trees above mentioned—"be planted around the garden, other trees will be greatly benefited by its influential air," so says the Hindu author, and no doubt he is perfectly right. These graceful nim-trees, with their leaves so like a mountain-ash, and their bunches of green berries, are among the most decorative as well as the most useful trees. In fact the nim may be called the eucalyptus of India, from all the uses to which it is put. Not only does their "influential air" benefit the garden, not only do their branches placed in large vases decorate so prettily Anglo-Indian drawing-rooms, but their dried leaves strewn under bungalow rugs and carpets keep off the dreaded white ants, and laid like lavender among clothes and along bookshelves they frighten away the rapacious, all-devouring cockroaches. Among Indians its medicinal uses are endless, and in illness boughs are hung over the door, very much as we in England might hang up a sheet steeped in a disinfectant.

The question of the garden soil was carefully considered. It was placed under three heads: ground situated at a distance from water termed "jangala," that close to water called "anupa," and ground lying between the other two styled "samana." These three soils were subdivided into six different colours—black, almond-colour, wheat-colour, red, white, and yellow: the black being sweet in taste, the almond-colour sour, the wheat-colour saline, the red pungent, the white bitter, and the yellow astringent. It would take too long to quote all the different trees and plants considered suitable to each soil. But the old writer closes with a remark, the truth of which all good gardeners who have had to struggle with bad soils will appreciate: "If any lasting and productive tree be found on a different soil from that to which it is adapted, such casual growth is accounted for from the four causes, namely, that underneath the tree there might be a hidden treasure, or the tomb of a sage, or that the ruler of the country is fortunate and auspicious, or by the unwearied exertions and good conduct of the planter."

Babar, in his Memoirs, gives a long list of Indian fruit trees commencing with the mango, of which he says with his usual observation: "Such mangoes as are good, are excellent. Many are eaten, but few are good of their kind." The plantain he considers of the next importance, adding: "Its tree is not very tall, and indeed is not entitled to the appellation of tree; it is something between a tree and a vegetable." His list of the flowers new to him in India is short: jasun (*Antiaris toxicaria*), asoka tree, kanir (*oleander*), keuri (*Pandanus odoratissimus*), and last, "the white jasmine which they call chambeli. It is larger than our jasmine and its perfume is stronger."

The new Mughal style of gardening developed quickly on being transplanted to India. It began to take on fresh features even in the few years of Babar's reign in the country. The water, as we have seen, became more and more the central motive, and many new flowering shrubs, fruits, and vegetables were introduced. But when Babar's grandson, the Emperor Akbar, set a precedent by his marriage with a Rajputni, Mariam uz Zamani, Princess of Jaipur, Hindu influence at Court increased rapidly. At Fatehpur Sikri the Rajput Queen's Golden House and its little garden can still be seen. This Princess was the mother of the Emperor Jahangir, whose first wife was also a Rajput Princess, so that Shah Jahan, the great builder, was by descent more Rajput than Moslem.

Although the Central Asian garden had many symbolic and traditional characteristics, and was so closely interwoven with Mughal architecture, the bostand (orchard) was the only practical necessity to a Mohammedan, and the gulistand (flower garden) may be looked on more in the light of a charming luxury, gracing with its pretty poetic fancies the stern material Moslem point of view, like the rose sprays waving over the sharp stone edges of the raised garden paths. With Hindus, on the other hand, a flower garden is essential, as flowering shrubs and trees are the first requirement in the proper performance of daily worship. Every temple and private house has its garden, for flowers and leaves are considered worthless as offerings unless they are picked in the giver's own domain. No wild or jungle flowers may be used. Manucci was much struck by the old temple gardens, and says in his *Storia do Mogor*: "At every temple of their idols (called pagodas) there is usually an annexed flower-garden, just as in our parish churches in Europe, without comparing the two, there are graveyards. This garden is not less worthy of veneration and respect by these peoples, for every day the officiating priests told off for the

THE MARBLE SWING (DEEG).

purpose gather there the flowers with which they adorn some idols and embellish others. Such gardens arc to them what some cemetery is to us where the bodies of saints lie, from which flows some miraculous liquid capable of curing maladies that cannot be benefited by ordinary and natural remedies, or let us say like some culturable land bequeathed and vowed to any one of our churches so that the corn produced may be applied for the use of holy men."

Among Hindus the customs with regard to flowers and trees are very beautiful. With them there is no echo of the long quarrel between man and nature, which lingers in Christian and Moslem minds as a legacy from dark mediæval times; and Hindus have felt for centuries past things whose existence we, in the West, are only on the verge of realising. India, however, is no exception to the rule that it is women who preserve intact the old religious observances; there, as elsewhere, it is they who keep old memories fragrant—so the Indian garden is above all the purdah woman's province. The day begins with the housewife's reverence, the *pradakshina* about the sacred tulsi bush, which is generally planted in an altar built for the purpose in the centre of the house fore-court. Passing through a Brahmin village in Central India, one is often reminded of some clear-cut, classic bas-relief, by the glimpses caught through open doorways of spotless white-washed courtyards with their tulsi altars garlanded with flowers, where the women, so stately in their floating veils, go about their work.

In every Indian garden it is necessary to have three kinds of trees—mango, jaman, and amalaka—the leaves of which are used in worship, and for decorations at weddings, and on the occasion of a birth. Among the flowers the lotus comes first, but every flowering tree is sacred in India. The splendid red blossoms which come out in February and March, covering the gaunt boughs of the silk cotton tree (*Bombax malabaricum*), are sacred to Siva. The dhak tree (*Butea frondosa*), the Flame of the Forest, which burns so brightly all through the same wedding months, is one of Buddha's flowers. The mountain ebony (*Bauhinia purpurea*) is one of the most beautiful of the flowering trees, with its large delicate mauve blossoms whose perfume recalls the heavy softness of gloxinias. The white variety is sacred to the goddess of Good Fortune and Beauty, the Lady Lakshmi, the consort of Vishnu, who himself has many flowers sacred to him beside his blue lotus. The chambeli (jasmine) is sacred to him, and also to Kama Deva, the Indian Cupid.

But the champaka, the "pagoda tree" of the old Anglo-Indian phrase "to shake the pagoda tree," is more especially Kama Deva's flower. It is essentially the tree of Cambodia, the place name Cambodia being in Sanskrit Champak. Jahangir puts it first on his list of Indian flowers, saying: "It is a flower of exceedingly sweet fragrance; it has the shape of a saffron-flower, but is yellow inclining to white. The tree is very symmetrical and large, full of branches and leaves, and is shady. When in flower one tree will perfume the garden." Earrings and necklaces are made from its sweet thick-petalled buds, and very bewitching the Hindu ladies look when they wear Kama's flowers. Recently the fashion has crept into palace zenanas of wearing pearl and diamond jewelry every evening. But formerly the ladies wore such ornaments only for special festivities, and decked themselves at other times with a sweet-scented flower-jewelry of chambeli and champaka buds. Almost every Anglo-Indian garden can show some of these quick-growing trees, with their curious india-rubber like stalks, glossy pointed leaves, and tufts of creamy flowers. Frangipanni, one hears it called sometimes, though I do not know why. No garden is complete in India without its champak tree, and the mali will plant one, should you neglect to do so, and ignore such an excellent omen. But be careful where he plants it, for the champaka is far too holy ever to be cut down. The images of Buddha are carved from the wood of its branches; and its little blossoms are still strung together to form festival garlands—those necklaces which look so quaint and sit so strangely on the black frock-coat of Anglo-Indian officialdom, and yet, despite their wearers' self-conscious faces, add such a touch of Eastern charm and dignity to the simplest ceremonial. Holy days and festivals are all graced by champak flowers; arrivals or leave-takings are marked by the presentation of these sweet-scented wreaths. Great scenes and stirring moments fade in spite of all our will to keep them fresh; while pleasant things, unnoticed from their very monotony, sink deep into the mind;—the white blaze of the sunlight, the sweet crooning whistle of the Indian kites, and the scent of the champak wreaths.

PLATE XXXVIII.

ON THE WAY TO THE SHALIMAR.

The natural divinity of trees, their fruit, the shelter they afford from the sun or bitter winds, their green leafy mystery, the sense of protection and consolation they bestow,—all this is felt more vividly in Eastern countries than in Northern climes, where people tend to drift away from earlier, simpler realities. Nature is not so near in England as in India. The cold which forces us to use our wits, shuts us in from many things.

So we have left *phytomancy*—the divination or speech of trees—and many other pretty things, now called by long names, behind us, and the garden, fond as we are of it, cannot talk to us as it can to Indian hearts which are still full of "the intelligence of the flowers." Krishna one day hid from his wife in the forest, and she wandered about seeking for him. Wherever she went down the long green glades, the trees drooped sadly, and the flowers hung their closed heads. At last she espied a tree in the direction of which a herd of fawns with large black eyes were grazing placidly, where the flowers looked bright and wide-awake, and birds were singing and flying happily from branch to branch; and there was Krishna fast asleep in the shade!

Though colour counts for much in an Indian garden, perfume counts for more. Flowers are not picked unless they are an "acceptable," *i.e.* sweet-smelling, offering to the gods. If used for decorative purposes, an offering of some of them is first made. This same religious sentiment is also carried out in other ways: a gift of jewelry or rich clothing to a child or to a bride or bridegroom being dedicated, as it were, in a temple before its presentation. A favourite temple offering is a bed of flowers under a little arbour or "house of flowers." The bed is made of sweet-scented petals strewn on a sheet, over the petals a fine muslin cloth is spread, and this is then considered "a bed fit for the gods." Unscented flowers may from time to time be placed in private rooms just to look at for the pleasure of their colours—probably with the idea of following a Moslem or English custom; but if scented flowers were gathered for this purpose and used without any previous offering, the Hindu idea would be that the flowers had sinned.

To inhale a scented leaf on waking in the morning is thought to restore freshness and health—surely a pleasanter prescription would be hard to find.

Water, trees, fruit, and perfumed flowers—this is the order of an Indian garden ; then come the birds. No conception of a Hindu or Moslem Paradise is possible without their bright daintiness and sweet little songs. The birds, too, for all their gaiety, are wise—shall we not rather say are gay because they are wise? Birds fly everywhere and know everything ; whence the old classic "Auspicium" or "Augurium," and trees are specially planted to attract them. Every garden should have its close dark cypresses for them to nest in ; for Kapolas the dove, and Cukas the green parrot of love, who shares with the Bignonia creeper twining through the lattice the honour of being Kama Deva's messenger. Kokilas, the Indian cuckoo, whose song the vain peacock tries to rival, never sings his sweetest until he sees the buds of the palace Asoka-tree burst into flower. He is the bird of the Hindu poets and teaches them melody—an odd music-master, to our ears. Vartika, the watchful quail, shares the grass-plot with the hoopoes, who are to be encouraged as much for their graceful shape and dainty crest as for their song, the prediction of a plentiful vintage. The red geese are Brahma's birds of sunrise ; and no garden can expect to prosper without the divine twins, the white Hanas, the ducks or swans of good fortune, swimming on its pools, and the butterflies of good luck, the souls of the departed, hovering in bliss over the flowers.

Many fresh and charming ideas stepped into the Mughal gardens with the first Rajput queen. But the greatest change the Hindu influence wrought was the introduction of the moonlight garden ; the change from the sunlit Turki gardens, with the glory of their blended parterres and red rose alleys, to moonlight Indian gardens of dark trees, white flowers, white paths, perfumes, and lights. The Hindu pleasance is planned essentially for evening enjoyment. Not that the Mughals failed to see the beauty of night. Babar, who so loved the glowing rings of the camp fires, had his Mahtab Bagh, one may be sure. But the Indian flowering trees being at their best in the hot weather and the rains, especially when the cool evening breeze brings out their perfume, Hindu ladies until recently rarely entered their gardens except at night.

In the fierce hot weather of the Central Indian plains the advantages and charms of the old baghs, with their cascades and swimming pools, are easily recognisable. Then, when the treasured winter annuals of the bungalow gardens are all burnt up,—those indifferent sweet-peas, minute pansies, and tiny violets, offerings of which the mali presents with pride; for does he not know them from experience to be the Sahib's sacred flowers?—when even the Phlox Drummondi and the sunflower fail, and only the petunias and the fountain are left alive to console each other and brave the scorching midday wind, how one longs for a real Indian garden! The heat shuts one fast in the house by day; and after nightfall it is not safe to wander on the grass or the dark gravel paths. The malevolent ghosts, so feared by the garden coolies, may not hide for us in the dim shapes of the trees, but other dangers lurk on the ground, for even in the clear moonlight a snake may be mistaken for a stick. And how can one seriously set out to enjoy the fragrance of some white-starred gardenia-bush, attended by the watchman with his long staff and lamp!

An Indian garden, a great series of outdoor rooms, is, on the other hand, a beautiful and sensible place in which to wander after dark as well as by day. The long stone paths, raised above the level of the soil and fringed by fragrant flowering shrubs, shine clear in the starlight. The raised chabutras, or pavilions, where the main paths cross have each their tank or fountain basin, and can be easily flooded with water and cooled; the little baradaris at the angles of the walls are open on every side to the evening breeze; and the flowers themselves in an Indian garden are chosen to look their best and smell their sweetest under the soft radiance of the moon.

An evening garden, naturally, means a white garden, all other flowers being lost in the dusk of their leaves. So, many of the favourite Hindu flowers are white, like the champaka and double jasmine buds used for wreaths. Among others are white poppies, tuberose, datura, white petunia, stephanotis, magnolias, and gardenias of various kinds as well as the night opening flowers, the white scented cactus (*Cereus grandiflora*), the moon-creeper convolvulus called soma-vel (*Calonyction speciosum*), which when in bloom makes such a magical effect, and the white lotus beloved of Hindu poets. "Every one has his friend and confidant; the sun which opens the pink lotus, closes the petals of the white," is one of their sayings; and Hindu heroes and heroines declare their love for each other as "like that of the sun and the day lotus, or the moon and the white lotus flowers."

The white blossoming shrubs were grouped to stand out against the dark masses of the encircling trees; but black and white are not the only shades in the moonlight garden, there is also the red flower of fire. Beautiful colour schemes carried out in lights such as those under the waterfalls at Pinjor in their red and green alcoves, form quite a feature of Indian garden-craft. And how pretty these are when lighted can be realised even from their rather clumsy reproduction in the coloured waterfalls which face the entrance to the Shepherd's Bush "White City." The parterres and platforms also are often outlined with tiny earthen lamps; on festival occasions the trees are hung with lights; but the fireflies, which are held to be under the special influence of the moon, are considered the prettiest of evening decorations.

As the gardens of the Imperial palaces are nearly all transformed or destroyed, one must wander in the great lower garden of Pinjor, or visit the garden-palace of Deeg, to see the beauties and realise the charm of the Mughal gardens of the seventeenth and eighteenth centuries. The chapter of Indian garden history which Babar

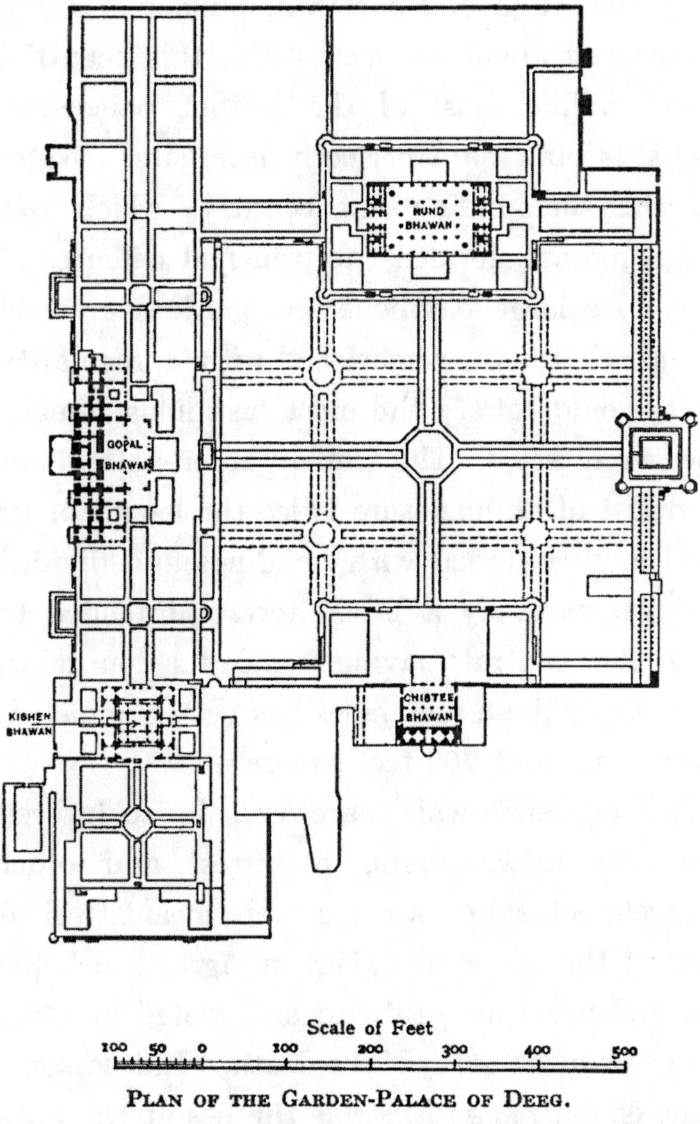

PLAN OF THE GARDEN-PALACE OF DEEG.

opened at Agra closes at Pinjor with Fadai Khan, but only to reopen with the story of Hindu palace builders, foremost among whom was the Suraj Mal, Raja of Bharatpur, builder of Deeg. Commenced about the year 1725, this beautiful palace, unlike most of the Rajput palace-fortresses, is built on a perfectly level site. Water and the surrounding flat country, which was once a morass, formed the principal defences of Deeg. Its large pavilions and gardens are laid out, as Fergusson remarks, "with a regularity which would satisfy the most fastidious Renaissance architect." The whole garden-palace was to consist of an enclosure twice the length of its breadth, surrounded with buildings and divided into two parts by a broad terrace intended to carry the central pavilion and its fountains. Only one of these rectangles has been completed, measuring about 700 feet square.

The gardens, which are rich in sculptured fountains, watercourses, parterres, and other fine architectural ornaments, were meant to rival those of the Imperial Palace at Agra, which the Jats of Bharatpur captured and looted in 1765, two years after Suraj Mal's death. Indeed some of the chabutras and marble thrones at Deeg are actually those taken from the Mughals. One wonders if the lovely white marble swing (Plate

XXXVII.) also came from the palace gardens of Nur-Jahan and her niece Arjmand, the Beloved. The principal building is the Gopal Bhawan; the north side of which faces a large bathing tank, and with its balconies and open pavilions forms a beautiful water front. One of the great features of Deeg apart from the gardens is the fine roof terraces. The flat Indian roof, "the best room of the house," is here extended on all four sides beyond the walls of the building by a bracketed pierced stone cornice. Below this again there is the usual wide dripstone; and this unique combination gives a large roof space for promenading in the cool of the evening, and the richest effect of light and shade to the buildings in the sunshine. February and March are the months to see this lovely garden-palace, Suraj Mal's fairy creation, at its best; when the fountains are playing, the flowering bushes are just coming out, the roses in the parterres are all in bloom, and the soft cool green of the mango, jaman, amalaka, and nim trees has not yet been spoiled by the hot, dusty winds of the Indian spring.

Although the Mughal garden under the influence of Hindu customs became essentially a moonlight one, yet there was one month in the year, Sawan (the middle rains), when the palace ladies went down to see how their gardens fared by day. There are few prettier places than an Indian "rains" garden, when the wonderful flowering trees and creepers are in perfection. The herbaceous flowers are limited, but those that do grow, grow so riotously that they quite make up for their lack of variety. One would hardly recognise a zinnia in an English border, after the great beds of coral, red and orange blooms with their large flower heads and branching stalks; each colour massed separately, in gorgeous parterres filled with zinnias alone. Tall cannas and balsams make another blaze of colour, marigolds and cosmos flourish, amaranth, orchids, and the orchid-like achimenes are out, the ponds are filled with lotus, and the wet garden glows and glistens where the light shines through the dark, damp masses of translucent coloured leaves, bushes of coleus, and tufts of caladiums, little pots of which look so dull in English greenhouses that one would never guess their splendour in the rains.

This month of Sawan—July—is the month of the swings. "It is both pleasant and profitable to swing in the rains," as I read once in some modern Indian book. In the damp, stifling air, when not even the watered fibre screens—the kas-kas tatties—can keep the rooms fresh, because there is no wind to blow through them, a swing under the trees wafts a cool, reviving air, and children and women, from the highest to the lowest, all have their swings. Sometimes it is but a rope thrown over the branch of a mango tree or slung between the pillars of a little court-yard, but in the palace gardens the swings were beautiful, elaborate constructions, their pointed arches forming one of the most charming garden ornaments. These arches were built of stone or white marble like that in the palace gardens at Deeg. They were finely carved, and when used in the month of Sawan were fitted with swings whose ropes were made of scented fibre and covered with wreaths of flowers. That at Deeg is placed on a platform under the trees at the end of one of the canals, where the swinger, swinging vigorously, could sway through the nearest fountain spray.

Swimming baths are another delightful and invariable feature of an Indian garden; and the ladies had their swimming tanks as well as the men. These reservoirs are shallow as a rule, and filled by one or more fountains, so that the water may always be running and clear. The canals were also kept clean and free from plants, the lotus tank being generally on one of the lowest terraces or in an outer garden. At the Lahore Shalimar the mistake has recently been made of trying to grow these flowers in the shallow canals, which only results in making the water muddy, and confusing the effect of the range of little fountains. On the other hand, if grown round the central chabutra of the large tank the lotus would look very well, for the plants themselves cannot be seen to advantage unless they are given plenty of space and deep water.

To return to the swimming pools. Certainly there is nothing so exhilarating as a swim in the open air; but among the changes due to the British Raj and the consequent copying of European fashions, one of the greatest drawbacks to Indian women must be the loss of their fine water gardens. Indeed, in India we all lose by the neglect of Indian garden art, but none of us lose more of health, delight, and happiness than the gentle purdah ladies, whose lives are, in truth, rather cramped by contact with our ideas when this entails the loss of their beautiful terraced roofs and pavilions, and the introduction of the open, exposed garden which they cannot enjoy. A recent instance will illustrate my meaning. On the outskirts of a famous Indian city, not far away from the old Mughal gardens in which I was sketching, fine new buildings for a girls' school were about to be opened. The school was a strictly purdah school—a comparatively new idea. The daughters and future wives of the Indian rulers and nobles were to be educated there, and fitted to become in after life good and helpful companions to their husbands and sons. By the particular advice of our wise Queen-Empress, their own best traditions and customs were in all cases to be adhered to. The opening ceremony was made an event of special importance. Princesses and officials' wives were gathered to meet the great lady who had snatched one day from a long round of other duties in order to be present. One could imagine how beautiful and useful the buildings to be opened might be—an Indian garden of girls; a modern maiden's palace, such as the garden-bower of Kadambari, the Gandharva Princess. One could picture the dark arched entrance; the main building with its cool fountain court and airy terraced roof; the pavilions and class-rooms built against the high enclosing garden walls; the swimming pool and the swings; the cypress walks, the squares of flowers and fruit trees, the plots laid out in grass for games,—the whole combining to unite the best of Indian and English common-sense and art with the pleasant freedom of complete security. And the reality? It was a large, solid, red-brick building of the British public institute order, with praiseworthy "Indian" trimmings by way of decoration, but with little Indian feeling; low walls, a gravel sweep, a dry, bare-looking garden, the whole surrounded with hideous matting screens—for was not this a school for purdah girls?

CHAPTER XII

SOME GARDEN CONTRASTS AND A DREAM

Heresy and Orthodoxy stand not behind the screen of Truth.
Heresy to the Heretic, Orthodoxy to the Orthodox;
But only the dust of the Rose Petal remains to the seller of perfume.

MAXIMS OF AKBAR.

THE history of the Mughal garden follows the course of other Indian arts. When Aurungzeb destroyed at one blow Indian unity and Akbar's dream of Empire, by the banishment of the Hindu craftsmen from the Moslem Court, they took refuge with the Hindu Princes of Rajputana and Central India. There the masons and master-builders of the Taj and the Mughal garden-palaces found welcome and generous patronage, as the splendid gardens and palace fortresses of the Hindu Rajas testify. It is in Rajputana, more than in the remaining Moslem centres of Lucknow and Hyderabad, or the great Anglo-Indian coast towns, that Indian art has survived the fall of the Mughal Empire and is still a living force. The pride of race and the immutable nationality of the Rajputs have combined, with the isolation and strength of their rocky and desert-bound country, to save Indian architecture and its dependent crafts from extinction.

But although "men come to build stately sooner than to garden finely," and Bacon's choice of the "greater perfection" is even more justified in the East than it is in the West, the garden, unfortunately, is the sooner altered and destroyed. Wherever English influence has been strong, as in British India and in the so-called "progressive" Native States, the typical Indian gardens have been the first to go, and the old symbolic garden-craft the first of all the traditional arts to disappear.

In place of the stately water-ways and avenues, the pergolas and gay parterres, the perfumed dusk of the Hindu pleasure-grounds, and the sunshine brilliance of the Mughal baghs, the incongruities of the Anglo-Indian landscape gardener reign supreme. It is easy enough to picture the change: the exposed private garden, a contradiction in its very terms; the public parks with their bare acres of unhappy-looking grass, their ugly bandstands, hideous iron railings, and forlorn

European statues; their wide, objectless roads, scattered flower-beds, and solitary trees, and, worst of all in a hot country, their lack of fountains and running water. It is pleasanter to turn to some modern Indian garden, an attempt, perhaps, to reconcile these two opposing styles.

In the station at which we were recently quartered, a wealthy merchant prince of the Jain caste happened to be rebuilding a large Anglo-Indian bungalow, and turning its grass compound into a garden. It was to be a country retreat, when the heat or the fear of plague drove the family from their high white palace in the town. And very interesting it was to see how they set about the work of reconstruction.

The position of the house prevented the idea of the four water-ways—roads in this case—being carried out in its entirety; but the first thing that was done was to run a path straight from end to end, replacing a former curving drive. A third road was then made leading up to the centre of the house, which from a solid block had been enlarged into a quadrangle enclosing a purdah garden for the ladies of the family; for the English fashion of the low outer walls would prevent their enjoyment of the rest of the grounds. At one end of the garden, under a line of fine old trees, several white marble shrines were built. These should have overlooked a large bathing tank, but the regulations of the station not permitting a sheet of stagnant water at close quarters to other bungalows, it had to be abandoned after being half dug out. And yet, had the tank been a shallow paved reservoir filled and refilled by fountains after the old fashion, there could have been no objection to it. But the only fountains in the garden were two large basins right and left of the main entrance, each surrounded by elaborate parterres made after the Mughal style, which is not yet quite forgotten in the gardens of Central India. In contrast with these was the round English lawn, presently to be adorned, so I was told, by a bust of His Majesty, the King-Emperor.

In another part of the grounds a terrace had been constructed decorated with chabutras bearing picturesque garden vases. These overlooked a large plot set apart for football or, perhaps, cricket. Then, across the wide mown lawns one came upon a quaint element of the old paradisiacal idea, the tame fawns pacing restlessly round and round, seeking to escape from their little white pavilions. Poor timid creatures, it was a tantalising Paradise for them, for there they were enclosed in the midst of an irrigated kitchen garden full of vegetables and herbs, where the tempting lush green leaves grew close against the pillars of their cages.

The garden "koti" grew day by day. Every evening on the road outside the little buggies whirled along carrying their drivers to tea and tennis at the cheery Anglo-Indian club. One heard various opinions on the new garden seen over the low wall with its ugly iron railing. Quaint, queer, inexplicable, or frankly hideous were the bewildered comments; but this garden, with its lovely parterres filled with white and yellow flowers, its marble shrines, its playing fields, and captive deer, if not artistically a complete success, was at least the most interesting experiment in the making of a modern Indian garden I had seen.

It was evident that the builder was trying to adapt Eastern symbols to Western fashions and ideas. It is not surprising to find Indians copying European styles even when their own are sounder and more suitable, as they naturally wish to imitate the arts of a nation which has proved itself to be so strong in other ways. But in these latter days of æsthetic revivals, and more particularly of the rediscovery of the truth that the house and garden should form one harmonious whole, it is indeed strange that we should be so slow to learn from India.

What useful and delightful gardens might be made for clubs, residences, and public pleasure-grounds in every Anglo-Indian Station, if we would but call the Indian master-builder and his malis to our aid. It would be difficult to find a more appropriate design for a modern Indian house, or palace and its grounds, than that of a Mughal bagh with its adjoining serai, such as can be seen at the Taj, or on a still larger scale at Shah-Dara, Jahangir's tomb. The open square of the serai would form a useful and dignified fore-court. The modern dwelling-house would take the place of the high entrance to the bagh; on the far side of which, the enclosed garden with its terraces, avenues, and long canals would stretch undisturbed. Apart from the beauty of Indian garden symbolism, and the use of the open pavilions and platforms, what a charm the formal setting and the fountains would lend to English skill in scientific horticulture—our ex-

PLATE XXXIX.

THE PILLAR OF VISHNU (FATEHPUR SIKRI).

perience in the actual growing of the various flowers and trees. Many detailed suggestions might be made, but that one subject, the problem of New Delhi, now absorbs all lesser interests of its kind in India.

Gardening, and its interwoven architecture, go to the very root of national life. In the garden the whole history of the nations finds a true and clear reflection. In times of peace and prosperity the craft expands and flourishes, while wars and long unsettled years sweep away the gardens and all their gentle arts. The Aryans of Vedic times brought their intense love of nature, their worship of trees and flowers, from the flowery tablelands and valleys of Central Asia to the Indian plains. After dim centuries, during which the priestly Brahman caste gained complete ascendency, and codes and elaborate ceremonies hardened and led to the creation of a chill, artificial world, the rise of Buddhism was welcomed and assured. The new phase of the old creed owed its immediate success to its restoration of the old joyous simplicities, and the "Lotus-bearers" of Asoka carried their flowers far and wide. Seventeen centuries later, with the coming of the Mughals, the wave washed back from the Central Asian gardens to India, where the peace and the genius of the Mughal Badshahi can be still traced in its baghs.

Since the fall of that Empire, raids and wars, years of unstable government and adverse European influences, have all but destroyed Indian gardening. Only in Rajputana and the lesser Native States something of the old skill lingers, something of the old fire smoulders. There it awaits the coming Indian renaissance. Whence will it come, that fresh breath which will blow the embers into flame? From new Japan? From the vast, slowly awakening bulk of China? Or from England? The British Badshahi which maintains the necessary peace, so far has lacked the intuition and taste to lead Indian art, and to trust to Indian craftsmen. But a love of nature generally, especially of flowers, is as much a national characteristic of the English as of Indians. Surely a fresh and brilliant chapter of Indian art and garden history should open at the Delhi of King George.

In the words of the town planner's recent report, "Delhi once more is to be an Imperial capital, and is to absorb the traditions of all the ancient capitals. It is to be the seat of the Government of India. It has to convey the idea of a peaceful domination and a dignified rule over the traditions and life of India by the British Raj."

But whoever its designers may be, however eloquent of the genius of individual Englishmen its plans may be, this last Delhi, like all its predecessors, will be built by Indian workmen. Ideas of "peaceful domination" or "dignified rule" are but a poor exchange for Indian religious feeling, for the deep traditional reverence of Indians for their Emperor.

The material advantages of our good government—peace, laws justly administered, education, sanitation, hospitals, even the fairyland of European science—leave the mass of India cold. But the return to the ancient capital commanded by the Emperor in person, made a direct appeal to Indian imagination and loyalty. The old Indian ideal of unity,—in BHARATA, the Holy Land,—revived and personified by their King-Emperor, touched the humblest peasant, and rekindled the long latent fires of Indian nationality. Here lies the great opportunity of New Delhi, for the motive that can really move and lead India must be a religious one. This truth is cut deep in the edicts of Asoka. It was a religious ideal that inspired the Moslem reverence for the older Badshahi. It was Hindu *bhakti* that strengthened Akbar's throne.

Religion, high politics, and statecraft may seem far enough away from gardens, but sound art makes for sound politics, and their affinity in India is curiously close. Akbar's pillar in his hall of private audience at Fatehpur Sikri is an instance of this in its strange beauty and its direct connection with the old ideas embodied in the sacred Mount, the Tree, and the Snake. On the outside the Diwan-i-Khas appears to be a two-storied building, but on entering it is seen to consist of a single vaulted hall, surrounded half-way up by a gallery. Standing alone in the centre of the chamber is a magnificently carved column, with a huge bracket capital which carried the Emperor's throne. The pillar supports four railed passages leading to the four corners of the gallery, where there were seats for the principal ministers. Here the Mount and the Tree are one, meeting in Vishnu's symbol of the Tree or Pillar of the Universe, whereon the Emperor as Vishnu's Regent sat enthroned; while the four passages symbolise the cosmic cross of the four-went rivers of the Celestial Paradise.

The Mughal miniature, Plate XL., said to represent Akbar as a young man, shows a garden throne or chabutra in a chenar tree. The symbolism of Vishnu's pillar is very literally carried out, and some such charming retreat in one of his grandfather Babar's northern gardens most probably suggested Akbar's novel treatment of the old idea.

It has been urged in connection with the planning of New Delhi, that "any departure in the direction of Indian ideals, even if it produce fine architecture—which is open to question—would be misinterpreted as a weakness, as a relaxing of the firm grip which maintains order." But whether we know it or not, whether we like it or not, consciously or unconsciously, whatever our official policy may be, we cannot escape in India from Indian ideals. Even the gold-embroidered umbrella of State held over the King-Emperor at the Delhi Durbar was but a symbol of the sacred sheltering Tree; a symbol greeted by the crowds who at sundown knelt in prayer before the empty thrones; and by those who, when their Majesties reached Calcutta, flung the welcoming marigold festoons into the Hugli till the sacred river blazed like an English field in the buttercup weeks of June.

The interest, therefore, of the new capital centres in the Badshahi Mahal, the Imperial Palace and its gardens — Government House, to give it the chill Anglo-Indian name. What are public institutes and pleasure-grounds, fine secretariats, alien Gothic cathedrals, Grecian post-offices, Roman forums, beside the Indian home of the Father of his people, the palace buildings of an Emperor who is Vishnu's Vice-Regent upon earth?

In a vast continent where temples, churches, mosques, forts, and even palaces but serve to mark and divide men and creeds, all might yet meet in a garden. Hindu and Moslem might both recognise their own symbols there, where the fountain mists and whispering trees would murmur to us of that power, the *bhakti*, which for all our restless Western cleverness we miss. There Indian women when they came to greet their Queen, or her representative, would each be welcomed by her own flowers and their legends, and the garden would speak for us better than we could ourselves. Laila would be there on her rose-bush mound or happy with her Majnum in the parterres; with scarlet asoka trees, Kama Deva's perfumed buds, and tulsi in the terrace vases; while the Lilies of Our Lady and the Lotus of the Good Law would share the gardens with the pink rose of the Persian poets and the red rose of England. Nor need we confine ourselves and our Indian craftsmen to imaginative reproductions of the past. New needs and our modern wealth of flowers would give fresh life and added beauty to ancient symbols and ideas, charms to rival and surpass all the older Shalimars.

The Mughal Imperial gardens consisted, as we have seen, of three large enclosures, opening one out of the other: the semi-public garden of the Diwan-i-'Am; the Emperor's garden with its Diwan-i-Khas, where he received his princes and chiefs; and the purdah garden of the Empress and her ladies. If the palace at New Delhi could form part of a scheme with a great Imperial Indian garden, with its symbolic divisions, water-ways, avenues, fountains, and walls, Indian art would receive a stimulus and Indian loyalty a lead which it would be impossible to overrate, although hard to believe in England,

THE CHENAR TREE THRONE.

(By kind permission of the Fine Arts Society, Ltd.)

where the gardens, beautiful as they are, lack the practical use and deeper religious significance of Indian garden-craft.

Far, and far, our homes are set round the Seven Seas :
Woe to us if we forget, we that hold by these :
Unto each his mother-beach, bloom, and bird, and land—
Masters of the Seven Seas, oh ! love and understand.

The Flowers—RUDYARD KIPLING.

Lo! ye shall read it in the Sacred Books
How, being met in that glad pleasaunce-place—
A garden in old days with hanging walls,
Fountains, and tanks, and rose-banked terraces
Girdled by gay pavilions and the sweep
Of stately palace-fronts—the Master sate
Eminent, worshipped, all the earnest throng
Watching the opening of his lips to learn
That wisdom which hath made our Asia mild;
Whereto four thousand lakhs of living souls
Witness this day.—

The Light of Asia—Sir EDWIN ARNOLD.

CHRONOLOGICAL LIST OF THE FIRST SIX MUGHAL EMPERORS AND OF THE PRINCIPAL GARDENS BUILT DURING THEIR REIGNS.

BABAR M. MAHUM, 1494–1531. Bagh-i-Vafa, Bagh-i-Kilan, near Kabul. Ram Bagh, and Zuhara Bagh, Agra.

HUMAYUN M. HAMIDA, 1531–1556. Humayun's Tomb Garden, Delhi.

AKBAR M. MARIAM-UZ-ZAMANI, 1556–1605. Gardens at Fatehpur-Sikri, Sikandarah (built on site of Sikandar Lodi's garden). Nisim Bagh, Kashmir.

JAHANGIR M. NUR-JAHAN, 1605–1628. Gardens at Udaipur. Dilkusha Bagh (Shah Dara), Lahore; Garden tomb of I'timad-ud-Daulah, Agra. Nishat Bagh, Shalimar Bagh, Achibal Bagh, Verinag Bagh, Kashmir. Wáh Bagh, Hasan Abdul.

SHAH JAHAN M. MUMTAZ MAHAL, 1628–1658. Shalimar Bagh, Lahore. Gardens in Delhi Fort, Taj gardens. Shalimar Bagh, Delhi. Dara Shukoh's garden, Kashmir.

AURUNGZEB M. DILRAS BANU, BEGAM, 1658–1707. Badshahi Mosque and garden, Lahore. Roshanara Bagh, Delhi. Chau Burji Bagh, Lahore. Nawan Kot Bagh, Lahore. Pinjor Bagh.

1725. Garden-Palace of Deeg, built by Suraj Mal, Maharaja of Bharatpur.

GLOSSARY

BADSHAH. A corruption of padishah, from *pad*, " a seat," " a throne," and *shah*, a prince—meaning Emperor.

BADSHAHI. Empire, imperial.

BADSHAHI MAHAL. Imperial palace.

BAGH. An enclosed garden, a country-house.

BARADARI. Literally " 12 doors," a pavilion, a large summer-house.

BHARATA. The epical name of India.

BHAKTI. Literally a state or condition of adoration, shown by devotion to altruistic works.

BOSTAN. A fruit-tree garden, an orchard.

BURJ. A fortified tower.

CHABUTRA. A four-cornered bank, a raised place or platform for sitting on.

CHADAR. Literally a sheet or shawl, here a water-chute or cascade.

CHAR-BAGH. Literally four gardens, here a large garden divided by four water-ways.

CHASMA. A sparkling [literally eye-bright] spring.

CHATRI. Literally an umbrella, here a small open baradari or summer-house; the word also means mausoleum.

CHENAR. The Oriental Plane-tree, *Platanus orientalis*, the fame of which has filled the whole history of Asia from the Punjab to Asia Minor from the beginning of human history.

GULISTAN. Literally a rose garden, but meaning also any flower garden.

HAUZ. A large stone-built tank.

HUMMUM. A bath, bath-house, a public bath-house.

LALA-ZAR or LALZAR. Literally a red garden, but meaning specifically a tulip garden.

MAHAL. A palace, mansion, house.

MALI. A gardener.

MELA. A meeting, a fair, also a fair held at the seat of some shrine for the benefit of the pilgrims.

MIHRAB. The central niche in the wall of a mosque marking the direction of Mecca.

MISTRI. A master craftsman.

PUJA. An act of devotion, of sacrifice.

SANAD. A deed or written grant, a charter.

SHIKARA. A small boat used in Kashmir on the rivers and lakes.

TAJ. Literally a cap, a crown, the word being the second syllable of the name of the favourite wife of Shah Jahan, the immortal Mumtaz-i-Mahal, the Ornament of the Palace; and her name being given to her sepulchral cenotaph at Agra, the word Taj gradually came to denominate any mausoleum.

INDEX

THE END